MOUNT RAINIER

MOUNT RAINIER

A Visitor's Companion

George Wuerthner

Photographs by George Wuerthner
Illustrations by Douglas W. Moore

STACKPOLE
BOOKS

Published by
STACKPOLE BOOKS
5067 Ritter Road
Mechanicsburg, PA 17055
www.stackpolebooks.com

Printed in China

Cover design by Caroline M. Stover
Cover photo by George Wuerthner: Tipsoo Lake, Mount Rainier National
    Park

10 9 8 7 6 5 4 3 2 1

First edition

Library of Congress Cataloging-in-Publication Data

Wuerthner, George
    Mount Rainier : a visitor's companion / George Wuerthner ;
    photographs by George Wuerthner ; illustrations by Douglas W.
    Moore.—1st ed.
        p. cm.
    Includes index.
    ISBN 0-8117-2856-0
    1. Mount Rainier National Park (Wash.)—Guidebooks.
    2. Natural history—Washington (State)—Mount Rainier National
    Park—Guidebooks. I. Title.

F897.R2 W84 2000
508.797'782 21—dc21
                                                99-046094

CONTENTS

ACKNOWLEDGMENTS

I received some assistance on this book from a variety of people with the National Park Service, including Eric Walkinshaw, Barbara Samora, and Rich Lechleitner at Mount Rainier National Park. Paul Schullery of Yellowstone National Park gave me some insights on early historical accounts of wildlife and of human endeavors on the mountain.

ABOUT THE AUTHOR

George Wuerthner is a full-time free-lance photographer, writer, and ecologist. An authority on national parks and conservation issues, he has written more than twenty other books, including *Yellowstone: A Visitor's Companion, Grand Canyon: A Visitor's Companion, Olympic: A Visitor's Companion, Texas's Big Bend Country, California Wilderness Areas Coasts and Mountains, Alaska Mountain Ranges,* and *The Adirondacks Forever Wild*. Wuerthner graduated from the University of Montana with degrees in wildlife biology and botany, received a master's in science communication from the University of California, Santa Cruz, and spent three more years pursuing a graduate degree in geography at the University of Oregon. He has worked as a university instructor, wilderness guide, park ranger, and biologist and currently lives in Livingston, Montana, north of Yellowstone National Park.

INTRODUCTION

On a clear day, from almost anywhere in the southern end of the Puget Sound lowlands, you can see Mount Rainier floating like a cloud above the Cascades, almost too grand, too splendid, too ethereal to be made of ordinary materials like rock and ice. Long a part of local Indian legends, Mount Rainier has always engendered respect and awe. To people living in the area today, it's a landmark that bears constant monitoring and commentary. Rainier is a daily part of life in the region. A common greeting in Seattle and environs is "Have you seen the mountain today?" "The mountain" needs no clarification—there is only one mountain that anyone is referring to.

Rainier is one of the grandest mountains in the United States. Its mark of distinction is its height, rising nearly three miles into the sky. The 14,411-foot summit is the highest peak in Washington, and the fifth highest in the lower forty-eight states. Few mountains rise as dramatically in overall elevation gain from base to summit. It was, however, once even larger. As recently as 75,000 years ago, Mount Rainier was estimated to be more than 16,000 feet high, with an even greater girth. A major eruption blew away the top of this volcanic mountain, and erosion has since stripped away much of the slope. Today the summit consists of two craters. The two vents overlap at Columbia Crest, which at 14,410 feet is the highest point on the mountain—and the goal of those climbing Rainier. On either side of Columbia Crest are Liberty Cap (14,112 feet) and Point Success (14,158 feet), remnants of the old cone.

Rainier is a well-watered mountain. Sticking up high above the rest of the Cascades, it intersects the prevailing westward-moving air masses coming in off the Pacific Ocean. Annual precipitation at mid elevations often exceeds 100 inches, typically coming as snow, which feeds the largest glacial system in the United States outside of Alaska. Meltwater from the snowy heights cascades off the mountain in more than 100 major named

Sunrise on Mount Rainier from Reflection Lakes.

falls. A number can be seen from the park road system, including Christine, Narada, Silver, and Box Canyon. To see the most spectacular falls requires hiking, however. Fairy Falls in Stevens Canyon drops 700 feet in two drops, making it one of the highest falls in the United States. Comet Falls spills from a hanging glacial valley, dropping 250 feet in two sections.

Mount Rainier is a stratovolcano, or composite volcano, like Mount Fuji, and is part of the Cascade volcanic belt, which also includes Mount Hood, Mount St. Helens, Mount Adams, and Mount Baker. Along the western edge of North America, the North American plate is overriding the Strait of Juan de Fuca plate, which is diving deep into the earth's mantle. At depths, the plate margin melts, providing the magma source for Mount Rainier and the other Cascade Range volcanoes.

Although it hasn't had a major eruption in several thousand years, the volcano is by no means dead. Steam jets, tremors, and occasional smoke all indicate that Rainier is still very much alive. Between 1820 and 1894, minor eruptions left layers of pumice covering the mountain. Today, the U.S. Geological Survey considers Rainier to be one of the most dangerous volcanoes in the United States. Its close proximity to Seattle and other Puget Sound cities means that any kind of large eruption could have serious consequences for millions of people. An eruption would likely melt the glacial mantle, causing massive mudflows and floods to surge down the surrounding river valleys. These flows would undoubtedly cause dams to break, sending the deluge toward Puget Sound cities. Mount Rainier is continuously monitored, however, and it's unlikely that any eruption would occur without warning. Nevertheless, even with monitoring, the eruption of Mount St. Helens killed thirty-six people, and if Rainier were to erupt, the loss of human life is still a concern, not to mention the potential for serious property damage.

In 1899, Mount Rainier was made our fifth national park. Today the park encompasses 241,922 acres. It's one of the smaller national parks—Yellowstone, for instance, is nearly ten times as large—but within its bounds are 382 lakes and tarns, five major watersheds, magnificent old-growth forests, and some of the most sublime flowery subalpine meadows in the world.

The park originally was a square 18 miles on each side, with the mountain at the center. In 1931, the eastern boundary was extended to the watershed divide at the crest of the Cascades, adding 34,000 acres and giving the park its odd shape, with more or less straight lines on the west and north, but an ambling, jagged line on the east and southeast, following the crest of the Cascades. The majority of the park (196,168 acres) is in Pierce County, but Lewis County contains 39,444 acres.

The park is surrounded on most sides by national forest lands. To the north lies Mount Baker–Snoqualmie National Forest, to the east is Wenatchee National Forest, and along the park's southern boundary is Gifford Pinchot National Forest. National forests differ from national parks in many ways. Logging, livestock grazing, mining, and other resource extraction are allowed on national forest lands but are typically prohibited within national parks.

Not all of the adjacent national forest lands are developed, however. Indeed, there are substantial roadless lands adjacent to Mount Rainier National Park, some of which are protected as designated wilderness.

These include the 14,300-acre Clearwater, the 50,923-acre Norse Peak, the 3,080-acre Glacier View, the 15,800-acre Tatoosh, and the 167,195-acre William O. Douglas Wilderness Areas. These areas provide undeveloped buffers on most sides of the park. On the western side, however, lies some private timber company land that has been heavily logged and is distinguished by the absence of large trees.

Some 228,480 acres of Mount Rainier National Park was formally designated as wilderness by Congress in 1988. Wilderness designation prohibits the use of motorized vehicles and most forms of intensive development, such as mining, logging, and road building. Recreational uses, such as camping and fishing, are permitted. Wilderness protection enhances wildlife and watershed values.

Approximately 2 million people visit Rainier in a typical year, nearly half of these in July and August. More than half of the visitors are from Washington. Most people drive through the park in one day, and Paradise is the favorite destination.

There are 161 miles of roads in the park. The first road to be constructed in the park went from the Nisqually entrance to Longmire. Later the road was improved to carry people all the way to Paradise. The Nisqually to Longmire section was first opened to autos in 1907, when sixty vehicles drove on it. It wasn't until 1915 that the public was able to drive to Paradise.

Other roads soon penetrated the park borders. On the north side of the park, the road up the Carbon River was finished in 1924, while the dirt road to Mowich Lake was completed in 1933.

The primary scenic road is the Mather Memorial Parkway, named for Stephen Mather, first director of the National Park Service. Part of State Highway 410, it follows the White River and crosses Cayuse and Chinook Passes en route to Yakima on the east side of the Cascades. There are lovely old-growth forests along the lower White River and spectacular views of Rainier up the White River Valley and from Tipsoo Lake near Chinook Pass. Connecting the Mather Memorial Parkway with the Ohanapecosh entrance is the East Side Road, which provides access to the old-growth Grove of the Patriarchs. The Stevens Canyon Highway follows Stevens Canyon and crosses the Cowlitz Divide, eventually connecting to the East Side Road near Silver Falls. The West Side Road begins near the Nisqually entrance and once ran as far as the North Puyallup River. As a result of flood damage, the road is now closed after less than 3 miles.

Paradise Park and Mount Rainier.

Once in the park, many visitors hike around the loop at Paradise Meadows or at Yakima Park at Sunrise. There are plenty of other opportunities for exploration, with more than 300 miles of trails in the park, including the 93-mile-long Wonderland Trail, which encircles the mountain. For overnight camping, there are 600 sites in five vehicle-accessible campgrounds and more than forty-one designated backcountry camps.

Climbing the mountain is the goal of a small number of adventurous souls. In recent years, 9,000 to 10,000 people have tried to scale the mountain—with less than half successfully making the top. A few people, primarily professional guides, have summitted the mountain more than 350 times.

Mount Rainier inspires awe and reverence in all who visit the park. As a national icon and landmark, the mountain has no equal in the Pacific Northwest.

CLIMATE

Much of Mount Rainier's allure—mist threading through quiet forests, the warmth of the sun in flower-splashed meadows, the changing pattern of clouds swirling about the summit—is a consequence of its weather. The mountain is located in a temperate maritime region. As any resident of Seattle can attest, this translates into a wet, cloudy, mild climate.

More locally, the mountain's position on the western edge of the Cascade Range and less than 40 miles from Puget Sound affects the regional climate. Winter temperatures are seldom very cool, averaging in the mid to upper thirties during the day, and summer temperatures are comfortable, averaging in the mid-sixties to the upper seventies. In a typical year, there are only two days in both July and August when the temperature exceeds 90 degrees.

But it is precipitation, rather than temperature, that probably most affects the visitor's experience of the park. The wettest months are November, December, and January, with an average of more than a foot of precipitation each month. From November through February, the park experiences cloudy weather at least 80 percent of the time. At higher elevations, snow begins to accumulate in November, reaching an average depth of 18 to 23 feet at mid elevations by March. The average annual precipitation is 77 inches at Longmire and more than 125 inches at Paradise. The White River Valley, located in the rain shadow of the mountain, is the driest part of the park. The Carbon River is the wettest, as it is exposed to the full brunt of storms coming in off the Pacific Ocean.

For most Pacific Northwest residents, the rainy winters are tolerable because the summer months are absolutely gorgeous, with many sunny days and mild temperatures. As the sun moves northward with spring, the Jet Stream shifts north with it. The Aleutian Low influence weakens, and gradually the North Pacific High comes to dominate the Pacific North-

Fog fills upper White River Valley. The east side of Mount Rainier lies in the rain shadow of the mountain and is drier than the west side; nevertheless, all parts of Mount Rainier get a considerable amount of precipitation.

west Coast. By July the North Pacific High is parked off the west coast of the United States, bringing stable, clear weather to the region.

July and August are the sunniest months, with sunny days as much as 40 percent of the time. Droughts of several weeks or even months occur most summers. These summer droughts strongly influence which plants can survive in the Pacific Northwest and are one reason why conifers dominate the region. Because of the nearness of the marine environment, heating of land is minimized, reducing the potential for rapidly rising air that creates thunderheads and lightning. As a result, thunderstorms are relatively rare here. Even during the height of the summer, only one or two thunderstorms a month develop over Mount Rainier.

The climate of Mount Rainier is controlled by three factors: the close proximity of the Pacific Ocean to the west, the huge mass of Rainier itself, and the broader climatic controls exerted by the shifting influence of high- and low-pressure cells in the Northern Pacific. Of the three, perhaps the greatest influence is the nearby presence of the ocean. Water has the ability to store tremendous amounts of heat and release it slowly. Puget Sound is a huge heat sink, storing solar radiation from the sun as heat and slowly releasing it to the surrounding atmosphere. This, along with the moisture and heavy cloud cover, serves to moderate the temperature.

Major climatic influences affecting the entire Pacific Northwest are controlled by two major air mass systems: the North Pacific High and the Aleutian Low. The center for the North Pacific High lies approximately 1,000 miles off the coast of San Francisco and is responsible for California's wonderful dry, sunny climate. The Aleutian Low lies off the Gulf of Alaska and Bering Sea. It generates wet, cool weather and frequent stormy conditions, as anyone who has visited Alaska's Aleutian Islands can testify. Where these two pressure systems meet, there is a prevailing westerly wind.

In winter the Aleutian Low intensifies and moves southward, bringing wet storm fronts to the Pacific Northwest. In summer, the North Pacific High advances northward, generating clear, dry weather. The shifting motion of these major air masses relative to western Washington controls the seasonal, and even the day-to-day, weather of Mount Rainier.

The reason for this variance in weather is due to how these different pressure systems operate. The North Pacific High spins clockwise, with the air mass traveling across the relatively cool waters of the North Pacific in the Gulf of Alaska. As a result, the air is cooled and is unable to hold much moisture. The Aleutian Low spins counterclockwise, traveling long distances over the warmer waters of the mid-Pacific. By the time the Aleutian Low frontal systems reach the West Coast, they have absorbed a tremendous amount of moisture and heat. Consequently, coastal lands bathed by these prevailing winds are warmed in winter and cooled in summer. In effect, the Pacific Northwest has a natural air-conditioning and heating system created by the Pacific Ocean and prevailing winds.

Occasionally, air masses from the interior of the continent climb over the Cascade Mountains and reach the Pacific Northwest. The temperature extremes recorded at Mount Rainier occur at these times. For example, it was during such a blast of Arctic weather that the record low of 18 below zero was recorded at Mount Rainier. Similarly in summer, hot air from the interior of North America manages to cross the Cascades, bringing high summer temperatures and drying winds. This accounts for the record high of 101 degrees recorded at the mountain.

In summer, these east winds bring not only warm temperatures, but also low humidity of 20 to 30 percent. Indeed, in crossing and descending the Cascade Mountains, these air masses warm and are able to absorb even more moisture. Acting like a sponge, they suck up whatever moisture there is in the landscape, further drying out the forests. The extended duration of these conditions often leads to ideal burning conditions and is responsible for the occasional large wildfires that periodically burn even rain forests.

The other major influence on the Pacific Northwest are winter cyclonic storms originating in the tropics. The Jet Stream, high-altitude winds that circle the globe, drag these storms to the Pacific Coast. These tempests pass over the Pacific Northwest, bringing drizzly, cloudy weather. At times, however, the center of these cyclonic storms will lash the northern California, Oregon, and Washington coasts, bringing record-breaking torrential rains and howling winds. The greatest rainfall and flooding typically occur at these times. Because warm air can hold a higher amount of moisture than cooler air, these storms often bring days of heavy rain. The abundant rainfall melts mountain snowpacks, and the warm tropical air accelerates the snowmelt. If the soils are already saturated, the end result is often extensive flooding.

The presence of Mount Rainier, a huge mountain mass, rising nearly 3 miles into the upper atmosphere strongly influences weather patterns. Air temperatures usually drop an average of 3.5 degrees F for every 1,000-foot gain in elevation. Thus, as you ascend the mountain, you'll find the air temperatures becoming cooler. The temperature at the summit of the mountain may be as much as 35 to 40 degrees cooler than at the base. The actual temperature change is contingent upon many variables, including the amount of moisture in the air and the temperature of rising air masses.

Clouds coming off the Pacific Ocean pile up against Mount Rainier. In climbing over them, these air masses cool. Since cool air can't hold as much moisture as warmer air, the clouds release this moisture in the form of great amounts of precipitation. The higher the elevation, the more moisture that typically falls, up to about 9,000 feet, where the increasing cold limits the ability of air to hold moisture.

Mountains also channel air movement. In summer, air cooled by Mount Rainier's glaciers flows rapidly down valleys, bringing nighttime cooling. During the day, warm air heated in the valleys rises, creating

Hiker on the trail to Berkeley Park frames the summit of Mount Rainier. Rainier is so high that the summit often spawns its own weather, as can be seen here.

gentle upslope daytime breezes and heating the upper slopes. Since cool air sinks, the bottoms of alpine basins are often significantly colder than adjacent slopes and terraces—an important consideration in picking a tent site if you don't have a warm sleeping bag. The cool airflow also influences plant growth. Many alpine basins are treeless while adjacent slopes have trees, because the cold air in the basin bottoms creates conditions too frigid for the successful establishment of tree seedlings.

AVERAGE HIGH AND LOW TEMPERATURES (°F)		
Paradise (5,400'/1,647m)	Longmire (2,762'/825m)	Ohanapecosh (1,950'/560m)
33/21	36/24	39/30
35/22	40/26	41/30
37/22	44/28	42/32
44/27	53/32	58/35
50/32	62/37	70/41
56/44	66/43	77/45
64/44	75/47	78/49
63/43	74/47	81/48
57/39	68/43	72/43
48/33	57/38	57/36
41/37	45/31	39/27
34/22	39/28	34/23

Month labels (left column): Jan., Feb., March, April, May, June, July, Aug., Sept., Oct., Nov., Dec.

in the region. By the early 1800s, both American and British fur companies had established a foothold in the region, building trading posts up and down the Columbia River and its tributaries. The greatest influence was exerted by the Hudson's Bay Company, which established Fort Vancouver on the Columbia River. The company went on to build Fort Nisqually on Puget Sound in 1833, expanding its sphere of influence to tribes directly below Mount Rainier.

The exploration of the Puget Sound region was occurring against the backdrop of increasing American interest in the Pacific Northwest. Beginning as a trickle and growing to a flood by the 1840s, tens of thousands of Americans seeking free land and the agricultural opportunities of the Pacific Northwest crossed the continent on the Oregon Trail to colonize the region. Many of these people settled in Oregon's Willamette Valley, but some, such as Michael Simmons, moved north of the Columbia River to settle in Washington's heavily timbered Puget Sound country. In 1845, Simmons founded the community of Tumwater on the southern arm of the sound.

During this entire period, there was wrangling between Britain and the United States over control of the Pacific Northwest. With the growing American presence, particularly in Oregon, the boundary between Canada and the United States was set at the 49th parallel, bringing what is now Washington State under U.S. control. Resolution of this boundary dispute initiated rapid settlement of the Puget Sound country. Seattle, Olympia, and Port Townsend were all established in the 1850s.

Early Mountaineers

One of the first attempts to explore Mount Rainier was made by Dr. William Tolmie, a twenty-one-year-old physician at Fort Nisqually who had just graduated from medical school. In August 1833, Tolmie left the fort with five Indians on a ten-day trip to collect medicinal herbs. The group followed the Puyallup River upstream to the Mowich River, and eventually into what is now Mount Rainier National Park. On September 2, Tolmie climbed to the summit of a peak "immediately under Rainier." Some believe this was Hessong Rock near Spray Park. Tolmie observed that the mountain "appeared surpassingly splendid and magnificent" and noted its glaciers.

In 1841, Comdr. Charles Wilkes arrived at Fort Nisqually with orders to explore the Cascades. Wilkes never got close to Rainier, but he made the first attempts to estimate its elevation, calculating it at 12,330 feet. His estimate stood for over forty years. Members of the Wilkes expedition, under command of Lt. Robert Johnson, crossed the Cascades near Rainier by way of Naches Pass.

In 1852, a group of four men, led by S. S. Ford, scouted for a practical route across the Cascades. The Ford party reportedly climbed nearly to the summit of Mount Rainier.

According to a 1917 secondhand account in the *Washington Historical Quarterly*, a party of two unnamed white men who were surveying the border of the Yakama Indian Reservation in 1854 took time off from their work to ascend the mountain. They hired an Indian guide, and together they traveled up the Tieton drainage and camped by Mystic Lake below Winthrop Glacier. From this point, they reportedly climbed the mountain in one long day. There is no official record of this climb, except for the Indian guide's oral account written down years later. According to the guide, the men told him of a lake in the center of the mountain "with smoke or steam coming out all around like sweat-house." This matches other early descriptions, and these features are not observable without climbing the mountain to its summit.

The next attempt to scale the mountain was made by Lt. A. V. Kautz, who was stationed at Fort Steilacoom on Puget Sound. Kautz Creek and Glacier, on Mount Rainier's southwest slope, are named for the lieutenant. Thrashing their way through dense forests of fallen timber and heavy brush, it took Kautz's party a week of exhausting travel to get from the Sound to the mountain. Eventually they made a base camp near the Nisqually Glacier. Kautz and his party set out for the summit the next morning, although it was drizzling. The clouds lifted that afternoon, and they were treated to unparalleled views of the Cascades, including Mount Hood, Mount St. Helens, and Mount Adams. That evening, they reached a point probably less than 330 feet below the final summit crest. The men decided to descend rather than risk spending the night. They were running out of daylight, and the rapidly cooling air had frozen the water in Kautz's canteen. This decision cost them the fame of being the first official party to gain the summit; nevertheless, they survived to tell of their near success.

Thirteen years later, in August 1870, Hazard Stevens (for whom Stevens Canyon was named) and Philemon Van Trump (Van Trump Park and Falls are named in his honor) set out from Olympia with another adventurer,

Climber inside the broad, spacious summit crater of Mount Rainier. Hazard Stevens and Philemon Van Trump made the first successful climb of the mountain in 1870. Arriving on the summit late in the afternoon, they spent a miserable night without food and blankets huddled in a steam vent to keep from freezing.

Edmund Coleman, to climb the mountain. Stevens was a decorated Civil War veteran and son of Isaac Stevens, first territorial governor of Washington. Coleman had climbed in the Alps and had also successfully ascended Mount Baker. Van Trump, who was secretary to the governor, became one of the most successful early climbers of Rainier, ascending the mountain numerous times prior to 1900. En route, they hired James Longmire as guide. Longmire would later be strongly associated with Mount Rainier, after he constructed a lodge at what is today called Longmire, within the park.

Longmire led them up the Nisqually River and into the upper Cowlitz Valley. Here they hired a Yakama Indian named Sluiskin as guide. (Sluiskin Falls by Paradise was named in his honor.) Sluiskin took the party over the rugged Tatoosh Range to Mazama Ridge. Coleman lost his pack and struggled back to the base camp at Bear Prairie, while Sluiskin, Van Trump, and Stevens continued on.

Tatoosh Range across Stevens Canyon. Stevens Canyon is named for Hazard Stevens, who along with Philemon Van Trump, was the first to climb Mount Rainier in 1870.

The climbing party camped near the Nisqually Glacier. Sluiskin believed that they would die if they tried to climb the mountain, but Van Trump and Stevens continued the ascent without him, climbing the south side of the mountain by what is known as the Gibraltar Rock route. They were bombarded by falling rock and had to move slowly across a number of crevasses. Finally, despite strong winds, they managed to crawl the last few yards to the top of the summit crater, arriving at the top of the mountain around five o'clock in the evening. Caught on the mountain in freezing temperatures without a tent, sleeping bag, or food, the pair spent an uneasy night in an ice cave warmed by steam jets, alternately roasting one side of the body and freezing the other.

The next morning, they began their descent. Van Trump slipped and injured his leg, but with the help of pack stock, the two men eventually made it down. They returned to Olympia, where they basked in the glow of their historic achievement. Van Trump later became a vocal supporter of the effort to designate Mount Rainier as a national park.

In October 1870, two geologists, Samuel Emmons (for whom Emmons Glacier was named) and A. D. Wilson, guided by James Longmire, also made the summit. Climbing from Cowlitz Park, the party essentially followed the same route as Van Trump and Stevens. They made the summit by noon and descended the same day, arriving back at camp long after dark, completing the first one-day round-trip climb.

Meanwhile, Rainier was getting more and more attention. The Northern Pacific Railroad lay down tracks all the way to Wilkeson along the Carbon River. From here, a trail built by Bailey Willis (for whom the Willis Wall was named) led to the Carbon Glacier in the northern part of the park.

In August 1883, a party including George Bayley, Van Trump, and W. C. Ewing, along with James Longmire and Indian Henry (for whom Indian Henry's Hunting Ground was named), attempted Rainier. Bayley and Van Trump both made the summit, and for the first time, so did now sixty-three-year-old Longmire. The most significant consequence of this trip was the discovery by Longmire of the warm mineral springs he later claimed, building a resort based around the springs and the mountain.

The fourth summit climb—and first ascent from the north side—was successfully completed in August 1885 by Warner Fobes, Richard Wells, and George James. They first tried to scale the mountain from Spray Park by way of Ptarmigan Ridge, but failed. They made a second unsuccessful attempt via Winthrop and Emmons Glaciers, but they had difficulty breathing and succumbed to altitude sickness. They made one more try the next day by the same route, and this time they successfully made the summit. On top, they found a metal plate with the names of Bayley, Van Trump, Longmire, and Ewing.

In August 1888, a climbing group lead by Sierra Club founder John Muir (for whom Muir Camp above Paradise was named), along with E. S. Ingraham (for whom Ingraham Glacier was named), A. C. Warner, Charles V. Piper, D. W. Bass, Norman Booth, and P. B. Van Trump became the sixth party to successfully reach the summit. The climb was notable for several reasons. Muir, after experiencing Rainier's magic and beauty, would later go on to lobby for national park status for the mountain. He was greatly taken with Rainier, saying that the mountain's flowery meadows were "the most luxurious and the most extravagantly beautiful of all the Alpine gardens I ever beheld in my mountain-top ramblings."

Sunrise from Camp Muir at 10,000 feet on Rainier's flank. Camp Muir was named for Sierra Club founder and conservationist John Muir. Muir climbed the mountain in 1888.

The idea of creating a national park centered around Mount Rainier had overwhelming regional and national support and met with little opposition. At the time that Rainier was being considered for national park status, few could imagine any negative impact from national park designation. Much of what was proposed as a park was largely rocks and ice. No significant mineral deposits had ever been found on the mountain. It simply couldn't be used for any other purpose but tourism. No one wanted to farm it, ranch it, or homestead it. Although some of Rainier's mountain meadows were grazed by domestic livestock, there was a lot more pasture available closer to the lowlands where most of the ranchers resided. And though there are magnificent forests on the slopes of Mount Rainier, timber interests considered these trees to be inaccessible and inferior by comparison with the huge trees growing in the Puget Sound lowlands, which had only begun to be cut. There was a feeling at the time that logging could never exhaust the timber supplies of the lowlands. No one imagined that the trees on the steep, inaccessible slopes of the Cascades would ever be valuable for timber harvest. Even opposition from hunters was minimal, as most of the big game in the West had already been hunted to near extinction.

Railroad, Timber, and Mining Interests in the Park Lands

Though there was no vocal opposition to the park itself, there was opposition to the park legislation because of riders attached to the bill that had nothing to do with the park. But park supporters got a further boost from an unexpected source: the Northern Pacific Railroad, which hoped to benefit from the tourist crowds visiting the park, and also to use the park designation to further corporate control of more public-domain timberlands.

Generous railroad land grants were made by Congress to spur construction of transcontinental railroads and to privatize public holdings. Much of the grant in western Washington was covered with dense and valuable stands of timber, but some of the sections overlapped Mount Rainier and other higher rugged portions of the Cascades.

On March 2, 1899, McKinley signed the legislation creating Mount Rainier National Park, the nation's fifth national park. This came at a high price, however. Within three days of passage of the bill, the Northern Pacific exchanged hundreds of thousands of acres of its treeless rock and ice railroad grant lands for rich lowland timberlands, much of which it then sold to Weyerhaeuser Corporation, a timber company. Within a decade, Weyerhaeuser controlled almost 2 million acres of the most productive lower-elevation Pacific Northwest timberlands, most of which it had acquired from the Northern Pacific Railroad. Much of the vast Weyerhaeuser timber empire that exists in western Washington today can be traced to the Mount Rainier park legislation.

This and many other land scams at the turn of the century explain why most of the best timber-producing lands in western Washington, once formerly public domain, are today in the hands of private timber companies. It's fortunate that the lands now held by the Forest Service, as cut over as they are, were generally viewed at the turn of the century as too steep and rugged to exploit, or they too might belong to the commercial timber interests.

The new legislation also permitted mining in the park. Miners had already been scouring the area for gold, silver, copper, and other minerals. As early as 1897, miners were exploring the Glacier Basin area for minerals. Between 1905 and 1908, more than 300 claims were located in the park. These inholdings seriously compromised the management opportunities in the park, and in 1908, Congress passed legislation prohibiting any future staking of public land in the park for mineral deposits. Still, taxpayers had to buy back the existing mining properties over a period of many years, and at great cost.

Though most of the claims were never developed, a few mining operations did persist in the park for years. In Glacier Basin, the Mount Rainier Mining Company constructed a sawmill, power plant, hotel, and other buildings. Ruins of this operation still exist. A second major attempt at developing a mine occurred on Eagle Peak. Between 1914 and 1930, buildings and tunnels were constructed on the site. A flume was built to carry water to a powerhouse near the Paradise River. The remains are still visible today.

Remains of old mining shafts, rusted tools, pipes, and buildings are visible in other parts of the park, including the sites of the Washington Mining and Milling Company and the Hephizibah Mining Company development, both along the Carbon River, and at the North Mowich Glacier Mine. In most cases, nature has largely reclaimed these sites.

Mining wasn't the only commercial use of the park during its early years. By 1899, domestic sheep herds were grazing in the meadows by Sunrise, and by the early 1900s, ranchers were using many of the foothills,

Mather came into conflict with conservationists almost immediately over how he chose to implement this.

One of the first changes in park policy Mather instituted concerned concessions. Even before he was officially director of the Park Service, he had met with Washington businessmen, including the presidents of two major local timber companies, to promote recreational development in Mount Rainier. As he did later in other national parks, Mather offered exclusive monopolies to park concessions if they would construct tourist facilities like hotels and lodges. In response to Mather's offer, the Mount Rainier National Park Company was established to construct the luxurious Paradise Inn at Paradise Meadows. Though this lack of competition irritated many in the lodging business, Mather probably would have had a minimum of conflict over his policy changes had he not given monopolies to all commercial transportation in the parks as well.

By 1922, the Mountaineers were becoming increasingly disenchanted with Mather's policies, particularly regarding concession monopolies and development in the park. When a hiking group from Tacoma arrived at the park boundary in a rented van and truck full of gear on Labor Day weekend, they were forced to unload the van and truck contents, load everything onto a Mount Rainier National Park Company vehicle, and walk the four miles to the trailhead following the concessionaire's vehicle. This fueled a growing resentment among the very people who had worked so diligently to have the park established.

Mather also promoted other policies that soon put him in direct conflict with the Mountaineers and other conservation organizations. At the urging of Washington businessmen, and responding to the growing use of cars by Americans, Mather pushed to develop roads in Mount Rainier. The first road to be upgraded and improved ran from the Nisqually entrance to Paradise, following an old wagon road. It was completed by 1915. By 1930, in an attempt to access every major section of the park, roads had been built or were soon to be completed to the White River, Sunrise, Carbon River, and Stevens Canyon. Among the proposed plans were the construction of a round-the-mountain loop road, a road from Paradise to Panorama Point, a tramway, and two landing fields at 6,000 feet on the mountain.

The Round the Mountain Road was begun in 1913, and plans for the road were completed in 1920. In 1924, Congress authorized funding for the road. A road northward from the Nisqually Road was constructed as

Sunset on Mount Rainier from Ricksecker Point, named for highway engineer Eugene Ricksecker. The Nisqually-Paradise Highway was the first road built in the park. The Park Service considered the upper part of the road too dangerous for some drivers and erected a sign saying "Boys under 21 and women will not be permitted to drive automobiles between Nisqually Glacier Bridge and Paradise Valley."

far as the North Puyallup River. But lack of money and a mounting resistance to development in the park stopped further construction. Since 1993, the West Side Road, as it is known today, has been closed by mudslides and flood damage beyond the first three miles. Whether it will be reopened remains to be seen, although many environmentalists would like to see it stay closed and maintained as a trail.

Environmentalists were becoming increasingly alarmed at the continued assault on Mount Rainier's wildlands by the Park Service. The Mountaineers began to publicly oppose Park Service concession and development plans. They were so upset by the Park Service's policies and passion for development that they resolved that the Park Service be transferred to the Department of Agriculture under Forest Service jurisdiction. In 1928, the Mountaineers sent a formal complaint to the Park Service charging that its road-building plans were excessive and opened up too much of the park to development and commercialization. They suggested that a portion of the park be left roadless and wild. That year, park officials called for the northern section and a portion of the western corner of the park to remain undeveloped, and it remains so today.

Nevertheless, development elsewhere in the park continued. In the 1930s, the Mount Rainier National Park Company constructed a nine-hole golf course at Paradise. To increase winter use, a rope tow was constructed at Paradise, followed by a proposal to build a chair lift and turn Paradise into a winter resort. The Park Service finally killed the idea in 1954, but the last rope tow at Paradise wasn't removed until 1973.

Not all attempts to open up more of the park to commercial uses were a direct result of Park Service policy. During World War II, ranchers tried to capitalize upon the war effort to get access to Rainier's meadows for grazing their sheep. The Mountaineers successfully turned back this attempt to open the park to ranching by volunteering to graze sheep on their front lawns if necessary to help the war effort rather than permit the park to be devastated by sheep.

During the war, Mount Rainier also became a training ground for soldiers. In 1941, the 41st Division Military Ski Patrol was in the park on training maneuvers. They were followed by the 15th Infantry, which spent months in the park on training exercises. By 1943, at least three military divisions were training in the park, including the famous 10th Mountain Division. Later, some of these men used the skills they had developed on Rainier to fight in the Aleutian Islands and in the Italian Alps.

The mountaineering experience of these troops led to renewed interest in climbing on the mountain after World War II. The number of climbers attempting to reach the summit grew from 300 a year in the postwar years to more than 500 a year by the mid-1950s. Climbers began to use Rainier as a training ground for ascents of the glacier-clad mountains of the Yukon, Alaska, and the Himalayas.

In 1963, Jim Whittaker, a climbing guide on Rainier, became the first American to scale Mount Everest. The new attention to mountaineering created by the Everest climb attracted even more climbers to Rainier's slopes, and by the mid-1960s, more than 3,000 people were trying to scale the mountain annually. By the late 1990s, this figure had risen to some 10,000 climbers. Most go up the mountain by the now-standard Camp Muir route from Paradise or by way of Camp Schurman in the White River drainage. Many are guided by the Mount Rainier climbing company. Of the approximately 10,000 that attempt to reach the summit,

Henry M. Jackson Visitor Center was built with Mission 66 funds, a federal program begun in the 1950s to update and improve facilities in the national parks. The futuristic style exemplifies the Mission 66 goal of "modernizing" parks.

slightly less than half make it, a surprisingly high success rate, considering the difficulty involved in ascending the mountain.

Some of the best climbers regularly bound up the mountain in record time—some taking little more than five hours to make the round-trip climb from Paradise to the summit. Other summit records include a seven-year-old girl who is the youngest yet to make the summit, and an 81-year-old man from New Jersey. Even the physically handicapped have gone to the top of Rainier. In 1981, twelve climbers, including seven blind people, two deaf, one mute, a Vietnam veteran with one leg, and an epileptic, along with guides and helpers, attempted to reach the summit. Nine of the eleven made it!

Wildlife Management

During Mather's tenure, he also instituted predator control policies in the national parks. Hunters and trappers were sent to Mount Rainier and the other parks to destroy predatory animals. The superintendent of Mount Rainier National Park reported that the "reduction of predatory animals in the park is very desirable in order that game and wildlife may be permitted to increase. . . . The animals classed as predatory and whose presence in the park is detrimental to game and other animals are cougar, bobcat, lynx, coyote and wolf." By the time this policy was reversed in the 1930s and predators were given full protection within the park, the lynx and wolf were completely extirpated from Mount Rainier.

Today's abundant elk and deer herds provide an opportunity for restoration of the wolf. During the 1990s, there have been increasing reports of wolves in the Cascades, particularly north of Snoqualmie Pass, including one successful denning just south of the Canadian border. Undoubtedly, with or without our help, Rainer eventually will once again be home to these predators.

One of the long-standing debates in park management concerns elk, large deer family members that can weigh up to 1,000 pounds. Few elk were recorded near the park prior to 1900, during early exploration of the area. From 1912 through 1934, elk from Yellowstone were periodically released in Mount Rainier National Park and surrounding areas. By the 1960s, there was concern that elk numbers had grown too large for the amount of habitat to support them and that damage was resulting from overbrowsing.

There is disagreement over whether elk are native to the park and whether they should be tolerated or treated as an exotic species. Most of the early accounts of the exploration of Mount Rainier prior to 1894 do not mention elk, though they do occasionally make references to other wildlife, such as mountain goats, wolves, and black bears. This has led some writers to maintain that no elk were native to the Cascades. Yet this doesn't necessarily mean there were no elk; their populations simply may have become quite low. Based upon a thorough review of the anthropological and historical evidence by historian Paul Schullery, it seems difficult to believe there were no elk. Though fish made up much of the diet of local people, elk hunting was practiced by many tribes, and early historical accounts mention encountering native people with elk meat and parts. Tolmie, one of the first whites to visit Mount Rainier, related an encounter with a group of Indians northeast of Fort Nisqually who "had an abundance of elk's flesh" in their camp. Elk hides were used by local tribes for garments and shields. Historical references to elk near Yakima east of the Cascades also abound. While none of this proves that elk inhabited Mount Rainier, it is difficult to believe that they would be

Paradise Lodge was built in 1917 by the Rainier National Park Company under a monopoly granted by Stephen Mather, the first director of the Park Service. Mather's tendency to grant monopolies to concessionaires was opposed by many former park supporters, including the Mountaineers—one of the organizations that had helped to establish the new park.

present in the lowlands east and west of the Cascades and not occupy available habitat in the nearby mountains.

With the introduction of the rifle, elk were heavily exploited, not only by native people, but also by miners, settlers, and market hunters. This heavy, year-round, unrestricted hunting pressure no doubt significantly reduced elk numbers in the Cascades, as it did throughout the West. In

The presence of active volcanoes is explained by plate tectonics. The earth's crust is made up of a dozen or so large, continent-size plates that move slowly about the globe, powered by convection currents of magma circulating deep within the earth's mantle. Plates collide, separate, and sometimes override each other. Volcanoes tend to be concentrated along plate margins that are either spreading apart or colliding.

Typically, the core rocks of continental plates, like those of North America, are composed of lighter rocks than those that make up oceanic plates, like the Pacific Ocean basin. When the heavier rock of an oceanic plate encounters the lighter rock of a continental plate, the ocean basin dives under, or is subducted beneath, the advancing continental plate. As the plate is pushed downward, increasing temperature and pressure melt the rock, forming magma. This magma sometimes rises up through the overlying continental rock to erupt as a volcano. That's exactly what is occurring now off the Pacific Northwest coast.

Mount Rainier and the other Cascade volcanoes mark the edge of converging plate boundaries. Plate boundaries are often marked by deep trenches like those found along the coast of South America immediately west of the Andes and adjacent to the Aleutian Islands in Alaska. There is also a deep trench immediately west of the Pacific Northwest coast, where a small piece of ocean basin, the Juan de Fuca Plate, is being shoved under the westward-moving North American Plate. As the Juan de Fuca Plate dives under the North American Plate, it melts, creating the magma that feeds the Cascade volcanoes.

Different plate motions and positions contribute to the formation of different kinds of rocks. Uplift leads to erosion and creation of sedimentary rocks. Colliding plate margins often create volcanoes and igneous rocks. Heat and pressure lead to metamorphic rock. All three major kinds of rocks are found at Mount Rainier, although the most common visible outcrops are igneous.

Volcanoes

Igneous means "born of fire." There are two broad classes of igneous rock: extrusive and intrusive. If magma reaches the surface of the earth to erupt from a volcano, it is an extrusive rock known as lava. Most of the summit and sides of Mount Rainier, as well as the other high Cascade volcanoes, are composites of extrusive lava and other igneous rocks. If magma solidifies deep in the earth, it is an intrusive rock. Granite is one example of an intrusive igneous rock. It is very erosion resistant and when exposed at the earth's surface often results in spectacular landscapes. Many of the West's most dramatic mountain ranges, including the higher peaks of the North Cascades, the Sierra Nevada of California, the Tetons of Wyoming, and the Sawtooth Range of Idaho, are made of granite. The ragged Tatoosh Range on the southern boundary of Mount Rainier National Park is composed of an outcrop of granitic rock.

Magma varies considerably in the percentage of silica. The amount of silica affects the viscosity of the resulting magma. A kind of magma that is low in silica and very fluid is basalt. Basalt is one of the most common rocks on earth, making up most of the ocean basins and large areas of the continents. Basalt possesses about 50 percent silica. When basalt magma erupts from a vent it is very mellifluous and forms thin uniform sheets. The Columbia Plateau that makes up much of eastern Washington and Oregon was formed from such fluid flood basalts.

If the magma is approximately 60 percent silica, it is known as andesite (named for the Andes in South America, where volcanoes derived from this kind of rock are common). Andesite is far less abundant than basalt, making up only 10 percent of all igneous rock on earth. Andesite volcanoes are common along subduction zones or places where the plate margins are melting and magma is rising towards the surface. Not surprisingly, since the Cascades are located by a subducting plate margin, all of the High Cascade volcanoes, including Mount Rainier, are predominantly andesite.

If the magma contains 70 percent silica, it is known as rhyolite. Rhyolite is also relatively rare, making up approximately 10 percent of all igneous rock on earth. Rhyolite lava is very viscous and barely flows at all. Unlike basalt, which is formed chiefly from oceanic crust, rhyolitic lava tends to originate beneath continental crust. If rhyolitic magma fails to reach the surface of the earth and cools below the surface, it becomes a class of rock we call granitic. Most of the continental base rock is composed of granitic rocks. Rhyolite is like cold toothpaste. It seldom flows at all; rather, it bulges up to the surface, typically forming mound-like domes. Sometimes rhyolitic magma is so thick it tends to plug up the volcano vent. Pressure builds and often leads to an explosive result that literally blows mountains apart.

The source of magma thus influences the ultimate kind and form of volcano that results from an eruption. Basaltic lava, because of its higher volcanic peaks in the Pacific Northwest, such as Mount Baker, Mount St. Helens, Mount Hood, and Mount Rainier. Rainier itself is less than a million years old. Its base rests upon the eroded roots of the old Western Cascades. Eruptions of ash and pumice, along with andesitic lava flows, have built up layer upon layer of the steep-sided volcanic cone we know as Mount Rainier.

Basalt columns on Van Trump Creek. Rapid cooling of basalt and subsequent shrinkage lead to the formation of such columns.

Paintbrush frames the Tatoosh Range, an outcrop of granitic rock, exposed by erosion.

Some the initial lava flows from Mount Rainier's vent were very fluid basalts, which filled the existing old, eroded river valleys. Some of these valleys were up to 4,000 feet deep yet were completely filled with lava. Because the resulting new volcanic rock was harder than the older material surrounding it, erosion stripped away the surrounding rock, leaving

Narada Falls, like most of the waterfalls in the park, is composed of a sill of hard, erosion-resistant volcanic rock.

these ancient lava flows in bold relief like the roots of a giant tree radiating out from the main trunk of the Rainier volcano. Today these old lava flows remain exposed as flat-topped plateaus, like the vast level expanse of Grand Park.

About 75,000 years ago, Rainier reached its greatest height—16,000 feet—and was even more massive than it is today. Gibraltar Rock and Little Tahoma Peak, remnants of the old mountainside, stick out above the general level of Rainier's slope, giving some indication of how much larger Rainier used to be. Other prominent knobs on Rainier's flanks, such as Echo Peak and Observation Peak, were formed more recently as secondary vents.

Whereas volcanic flows built up Rainier, glaciers have worked to tear it down. Rainier's mantle of glaciers has excavated much of the original symmetrical cone, removing an estimated third of the mountain.

Mass Wasting

Other geological events have also altered the mountain's surface, although less dramatically. Mass wasting, where part of the mountain slumps or falls away, occurs with relative frequency on Rainier. These aren't disasters but are natural disturbances that create new habitat and opportunities for wildlands and plants. There are several different, but similar, forms of mass wasting that regularly occur on Mount Rainier.

Debris flows are one of the more common phenomena and regularly sweep Rainier's slopes. Most are triggered by outburst floods caused by the sudden release of water trapped in a glacier. The largest debris flow to occur since the establishment of the park swept down Kautz Creek in October 1947. Heavy rains precipitated a huge outburst flood from the Kautz Glacier, which rocketed a series of mudflows more than 5 miles down the Kautz Creek Valley. The Nisqually-Longmire Road (State Route 706) was buried under 28 feet of mud and debris. Dead trees and snags from this flood are easily viewed from the West Side Road.

The Nisqually River drainage also has been swept by debris flows numerous times in this century, sometimes destroying bridges built across the river canyon. Debris flows poured down the Nisqually River in 1926, 1932, 1934, 1955, 1968, 1970, 1972, and 1985.

Debris flows triggered by outburst floods have been even more common on Tahoma Creek. In 1967, a massive debris flow completely buried the Tahoma Creek Campground. Fortunately, the campground had been

Mudflows or lahars resulting from rapidly melting glaciers are one of the great-
est geological hazards on the mountain. Since 1967 more than twenty mudflows
have swept down Tahoma Creek, seen here, burying forests, part of the West
Side Road, and even a campground.

evacuated the day before because of a forest fire, so there were no casual-
ties. At least thirty-four debris flows have scoured Tahoma Creek in the
years since.

Outburst floods are unpredictable and are fairly common along the
glacial river valleys in the park. Should you encounter rapidly rising water
in a stream or hear a loud sound like a locomotive coming down a drainage, get to higher ground quickly. Debris flows move rapidly and can easily
overtake a hiker.

More dramatic mudflows typically associated with volcanoes are known
as lahars. At least fifty-five lahars have swept down the slopes of Mount
Rainier since the last ice age. Lahars are formed when water from heavy
rains or the rapid melting of a glacier, as occurs during a volcanic eruption, mixes with loose debris, mud, and ash to form a moving wave of mud
and water with the consistency of wet cement. Lahars can travel up to
fifty miles per hour. Such flows can sweep away everything in their path,
including large boulders and entire forests.

The largest known lahar on Mount Rainier was the Osceola Mudflow, which occurred 5,700 years ago when the northeast summit of the mountain collapsed. A huge landslide removed the top 2,000 feet of the volcano. This debris mixed with water and swept rapidly down the White River Valley, flowing for seventy miles all the way to Puget Sound near Auburn and Sumner.

Another lahar, known as the Electron Mudflow, occurred approximately 550 years ago. It swept down the Puyallup River Valley at fifty miles per hour, knocking down forests and covering everything in its path with mud dozens of feet deep. Though much smaller than the Osceola flow, it inundated thirty-six square miles of the Puget Sound lowlands.

If a mudflow of the scale and size of the Osceola flow occurred today, it could potentially wipe out entire towns and cities. Such a mudflow could be one of the largest and most destructive natural disasters in Washington history.

Mount Rainier's Glaciers

One of the most striking visual aspects of Mount Rainier is its icy mantle, which gives the mountain its look of great majesty. Glaciers have deeply excavated and furrowed the summit cone of Rainier. The cleavers, or rock ridges, that separate glaciers on Mount Rainier are outcrops of the original mountain surface that lie between the pockets cradling glacial ice. Mount Tahoma, on Rainier's flank, is another outcrop of the mountain's original preglacial slope.

Glaciers and permanent snowfields make up about 9 percent of the total park area. The snow and glaciers on Rainier are greater in volume than all other Cascade Range volcanoes combined. These icy rivers are huge reservoirs of fresh water and contain as much water as all the state's lakes, rivers, and reservoirs put together.

Rainier has twenty-six named glaciers and fifty small glaciers and snowfields. There are eleven primary glaciers: Nisqually, Ingraham, Carbon, Emmons, Kautz, Winthrop, North Mowich, South Mowich, Puyallup, Tahoma, and South Tahoma. Of the mountain's named glaciers, the 4½-mile-long Carbon Glacier is the thickest (700 feet) and reaches the lowest elevation (3,000 feet) of any glacier in the lower forty-eight states. The six-mile-long Emmons Glacier, in Rainier's White River Valley, is the largest single glacier in the lower forty-eight and blankets the northeast corner of the mountain.

Emmons Glacier is the largest glacier in the continental U.S. Mount Rainier has twenty-six major glaciers and fifty smaller ones, covering 9 percent of the total park area.

Glaciers are formed when more snow falls in winter than can melt in summer. The great quantities of snow that fall on Rainier's slope each year feed the mountain's immense glacial system. Some western slopes of the mountain are buried under as much as 100 feet of snow annually. Interestingly, the greatest snowfall occurs at mid elevations, not at the top of the mountain. Six major glaciers—Emmons, Ingraham, Nisqually, Winthrop, Kautz, and Tahoma—have their origins on Rainier's summit. The rest begin in the belt of greatest snowfall at mid elevations.

Glacial ice is created when snow compacts and crystallizes into ice, eventually oozing downhill. Most glaciers appear static, and indeed, they don't move rapidly. One of the maximum speeds recorded for any glacier was in May 1970, when the Nisqually Glacier galloped ahead more than twenty-nine inches in a single day. Because friction slows the ice along the glacier's margins, the center and top of a glacier advance more rapidly than the sides, giving rise to the typical tonguelike shape. The bottom of a glacier is under so much pressure that the ice becomes almost plastic, oozing along the underlying ground surface. The surface, however, is under less pressure, and if the glacier flows over a steep cliff or other obstruction, it cracks, forming crevasses. Crevasses are seldom more than 150 feet deep, since pressures at greater depths force them closed. For climbers traveling on glaciers, crevasses pose a serious and dangerous obstacle, especially if they are hidden by snow.

The advances and retreats of glaciers are regulated by climatic conditions. If more snow falls during a period of years than melts in summer, the glacier expands and advances. Less snow results in glacial retreat. During the past 75,000 years, there have been three major glacial ice-age advances and retreats of Rainier's glaciers, which were once much larger. At one time, the Colwitz Glacier extended well beyond Packwood, all the way to present-day Mossyrock, some sixty-five miles from its source on Rainier's flanks. During the most recent ice-age glacial advance, between 25,000 and 15,000 years ago, Rainier's glaciers reached their greatest size. At this time, nearly the entire area of the park was under glacial ice, which extended down the river valleys far beyond the current park boundaries. The Nisqually Glacier terminus was near the site of Alder Lake Dam, some thirty miles from the mountain.

After the last ice age ended some 10,000 years ago, most of Rainier's glaciers shrank. Then, between the fourteenth century and 1850, the glaciers advanced again. The Nisqually Glacier advanced more than 800 feet beyond the Glacier Bridge, and the Emmons Glacier advanced to within 1.2 miles of the current White River Campground. Between 1850 and 1950, Rainier's glaciers lost approximately one-quarter of their length. This retreat was reversed briefly between 1950 and the 1980s, when many of Rainier's larger glaciers advanced once more. The Emmons Glacier recovered some of the area it lost since the 1850s glacial maximum, and between 1965 and 1992, the Nisqually Glacier advanced and retreated three times.

Effects of Glaciation

With their great weight and bulk and their movement, glaciers have tremendous erosive power. A glacier grinds, bulldozes, and carries rock and other debris down the mountainside. Glaciers smooth and grind the surface of bedrock they pass over, giving it a glassy, polished appearance. Rocks and boulders embedded in the bottom of a glacier often act as a file, scraping the bedrock and leaving unidirectional scratches on the sur-

Like many of the smaller lakes in the park, the basin occupied by Tipsoo Lake was formed by a glacier.

Located across from the White River Valley, these U-shaped valleys were created by a grinding mass of glacial ice.

face called striations. Since these striations mark the general direction of glacial flow, naturalist John Muir called them the tracks of glaciers.

As a glacier moves downhill, it plucks boulders and rock from the bedrock and carves out bowl-shaped basins known by the French word *cirque* (pronounced "sirk"). If the glacier melts away, water frequently fills these basins, creating cirque lakes. Nearly all of the small lakes that dot the Mount Rainier landscape, such as Mowich, Tipsoo, and Crescent, are of glacial cirque origins. Many of the higher cirques on Rainier are still filled with glacial ice. The largest cirque on Mount Rainier—indeed, on any Cascade mountain—is Willis Wall at the head of the Carbon Glacier, measuring more than a mile and a half across.

The continual grinding of bedrock and other debris by the glacier creates a fine powdered rock called glacial flour. Glacial flour suspended in water gives glacial lakes a bluish turquoise color and makes glacial rivers, like the aptly named White River, an opaque milky white.

As a glacier moves down a valley, it continues to grind and sculpt the surrounding mountainsides. Over time, this steepens the sides of the valley and flattens out the floor, creating a characteristic U-shaped valley.

Glacial moraine, seen here in a side hill along the Ohanapecosh River, is identified by the random unsorted mix of large boulders within a matrix of smaller rocks and sand.

All the rock that glaciers are moving downhill accumulates in the front and along the sides of the glacier. This loose, unsorted debris is known as moraine. Rockpiles along the side of a glacier are called lateral moraines, while those at the terminus are known as terminal moraines. Moraines can also form dams, creating lakes. Mystic Lake by Mineral Mountain is one such lake.

Geological forces are still changing the Mount Rainier environment, all at different time scales. Avalanches and mudflows occur nearly every year someplace on the mountain, glaciers advance and retreat over centuries, and plate motion changes the face of the planet over millions of years. In essence, the Mount Rainier landscape is continuously evolving, giving a continually fresh but familiar face to the mountain.

PLANTS

Even without the magnificence of the mountain, Rainier's plant communities would be reason enough to make the area a national park. It is cloaked in some of the most magnificent coniferous forests found on earth and has the most spectacular wildflower gardens in the Pacific Northwest. Mount Rainier is host to 787 native plants and 107 exotic plant species. Mount Rainier is not geographically isolated from the rest of the Cascade Range and has developed few endemic species. There are only three endemic species: *Taushia stricklandii, Castilleja cryptantha, Pedicularis rainierensis.*

Although Mount Rainier is the most glaciated peak in the lower forty-eight states, some 57 percent of the park is forested. As a contrast to the heavily logged forests on its borders, the park protects a significant representation of the virgin Cascade Range forest, which is increasingly rare outside of a few national parks and wilderness areas.

There are a number of factors that broadly influence what grows where: elevation, precipitation, temperature, aspect, and past disturbances, such as wildlife or mudflows. Perhaps the most important influence upon plant community structure is elevation and its effects on temperature and snowfall. With a broad elevation range from 1,700 to over 14,000 feet, Mount Rainier provides a variety of climatic conditions for plant growth. As a rule, the higher the elevation, the cooler the temperatures. Plants with little tolerance for freezing are limited to the lower elevations of the park, while hardier plants that can take freezing temperatures and heavy snowfall can be found higher.

The amount of precipitation, particularly the snowpack depth, also affects plant distribution. The typically deep snowpack at mid elevations, often exceeding 15 to 20 feet, restricts what can grow there. By the time the snow melts in summer, the remaining growing season is so short that

Near the timberline, trees take on a stunted, wind-sheared appearance known as krummholtz.

only a relatively few species of plants can complete their life cycle. Precipitation on Mount Rainier increases with elevation up to about 8,000 to 9,000 feet, above which it begins to decline.

As a result of the effects of altitude on growing season, moisture, and temperature, the park's plant communities are broken down into three major zones: low-elevation forest (1,700 to 2,500 feet), mid-elevation forest (2,500 to 4,500 feet), and subalpine meadows and forest glades up to timberline (4,500 to 6,500 feet). Glaciers, snowfields, and rock dominate areas above 8,200 feet.

These broad plant community classifications are influenced on a microclimate basis by many other factors. South slopes are warmer and have a longer growing season than north slopes. A plant that is found up to 5,000 feet on a north slope might reach 6,000 feet on a sunny south-facing slope. Wetter and drier parts of the park also create microclimates with different plant communities. Forests reach up to about 5,250 feet on the snowier western slope but extend their range up beyond 6,000 feet in the rain shadow on the eastern side of the mountain, which is not only slightly drier, but also colder. Here are found some Rocky Mountain species not typically found in the rest of the park, such as Englemann spruce and lodgepole pine. The Ohanapecosh Valley in the southwest corner of the park, which is drier than the western side of the mountain and has more wildfires, is dominated by the fire-adapted Douglas fir. The Carbon River Valley, which has the wettest, mildest climate in the park and seldom burns, hosts Sitka spruce, a species normally found growing only near the coast.

One obvious feature about Mount Rainier's forests is the dominance by conifers. This is a result of climatic conditions. In the Pacific Northwest, despite the abundance of rainfall all winter, monthly precipitation falls to nearly zero during the summer and drought is common. In the mild, wet Pacific Northwest climate, conifers, which retain their needles year-round, are able to photosynthesize whenever there is enough moisture and temperatures are above freezing, which includes a significant portion of the fall and spring. In addition, conifers are drought tolerant. The needles have waxy coatings to reduce moisture loss and the ability to maintain internal cell water pressure against drying winds. Additionally, some conifer species have special adaptations to fire, a frequent occurrence due to the dry summers. Because of their need for a dependable water supply, most Pacific Northwest deciduous trees, such as big-leaf maple, cottonwood, and alder, are restricted to streamsides and seeps.

Low-Elevation Forests

The first thing most visitors notice on entering the park is the large trees. Mount Rainier's lower-elevation forests have magnificent old-growth Douglas fir, western red cedar, and western hemlock. Other associated tree species include the deciduous big-leaf maple, black cottonwood, and red alder along rivers. Dominant understory plants are the thorny devil's club, thimbleberry, vanilla leaf, oak fern, vine maple, and the evergreen sword fern. In the wet Carbon River Valley, Sitka spruce is found, while in the drier White River Valley, grand fir is intermixed with the other common conifer tree species.

These forests are among the densest, most luxuriant, and most productive coniferous forests on earth, and the dominant tree species are among

Hiker views giant western red cedar in the Patriarch Grove.

the longest-lived and largest tree species found anywhere. Old-growth Douglas fir and western red cedar occasionally reach more than 1,000 years of age, heights of more than 250 feet, and diameters of 10 or 12 feet.

Mid-Elevation Forests

Between 2,500 and 4,000 feet lie the Pacific silver fir mid-elevation forests. Though Douglas fir, western red cedar, and western hemlock may still occur, there are fewer as the elevation increases, until most sites are dominated by silver fir. In areas where fires have occurred, noble fir sometimes dominates a site for several hundred years before being overtaken by silver fir. In the understory, Alaska, black, oval-leaf, and red huckleberry are common. Other associated species include white rhododendron and goatsbeard.

Subalpine Forests

Between 4,000 feet and timberline (around 5,000 to 6,000 feet) grow trees adapted to heavy snow. Most have flexible branches and a narrow profile that reduces damage from snow. Here are found mountain hemlock, subalpine fir, Alaska yellow cedar, and whitebark pine. Few of these species are abundant enough to form continuous forests, but grow as patches of trees amid meadows and snowfields. There are some differences in distribution among the species. Subalpine fir and whitebark pine are largely restricted to drier, warmer locations and are most common in the eastern and northeastern parts of the park. Nearly pure stands of subalpine fir grow in the upper basins of the Ohanapecosh and White River drainages. Whitebark pine grows best on rocky, wind-blown ridges where snow cover is not excessive. Associated understory species include beargrass and avalanche and glacier lilies.

Wind-trimmed subalpine fir in Spray Park.

Autumn leaves of huckleberry turn subalpine meadow russet.

Subalpine Meadows

The subalpine meadows at Mount Rainier are the largest and most spectacular in the entire Cascade Range. Beginning with the first snowmelt and continuing uninterrupted until the end of August, a colorful floral quilt blankets Rainier's slopes with fragrant blossoms.

Meadows are maintained amid what would otherwise be forested slopes for a variety of reasons. Typically, flowers dominate where snow lies deep.

Trees require at least a two-month growing season. In many of the higher elevations of Mount Rainier, the time between snowmelt and new snowfall is so short that trees can't survive. In many subalpine settings, trees grow on the higher ridges and slopes where snow depth is lower, while flowers dominate the basins where snow collects. Cold air drainage can also limit tree growth. Cold air coming off Rainier's glaciers collects in basins. Even if they are snowfree, the basins may be so cold that tree seedlings can't become established.

Flowers crowd stream in Berkeley Park.

Red paintbrush frames Tatoosh Range.

The wide variety of flowers found in the subalpine-alpine meadows includes speedwell, phlox, pink mountain heather, yellow mountain heather, dwarf lupine, Tolmie's saxifrage, beargrass, spring beauty, Sitka valerian, western anemone, buttercup, monkey flower, glacier lily, scarlet paintbrush, bluebells, and a variety of asters and daisies.

Many of Rainier's meadows, including Indian Henry's Hunting Ground, Van Trump Park, Spray Park, and Paradise Meadows, have been invaded by trees as a result of climatic changes. During the major drought that gripped the West between 1928 and 1937, the normally deep snowpack diminished sufficiently to permit seedlings of subalpine fir and mountain hemlock to become established. While these trees are now maturing, a return to greater snowfall has prevented any further trees from growing in these meadows.

Old-Growth Forests

One of the unique attributes of Pacific Northwest forests is their great age. In the past, foresters looked on such forests as decadent and overmature because the volume of timber produced slows with age. Today, ecologists have come to recognize them as valuable ancient forests.

Forests dominated by large, old trees have certain unique characteristics not found in younger forest stands. The idea that managed forests mimic natural forests lacks ecological perspective. Indeed, commercial forests dedicated to timber production are not an adequate substitute for natural old-growth forest stands. In fact, the continued existence of forests in the Pacific Northwest, not to mention salmon and a host of other wildlife, may be dependent upon the existence and restoration of ancient forest ecosystems.

Unlike managed forests, which tend to be dominated by one age class, old-growth forests are characterized by multiple age classes. A typical unmanaged old-growth forest consists of large canopy trees, with midlevel understory species and a variety of shrubs. Snags and rotten logs are abundant. This creates more diversity in structural components, fostering greater diversity of plant and animal species associated with such forests. It is also an insurance policy for the forest, since diseases, insects, and even fires seldom attack or affect all age classes or species.

The structural function of old-growth forests is critical to many species. For instance, the spotted owl, center of forest policy controversy in the Pacific Northwest, relies upon the large branches found only in big old trees for shelter from the elements. Old-growth forests provide shade from the summer sun and protection from winter rainstorms. In addition, the spotted owl's major food source, flying squirrels, requires the cavities that are numerous in the snags and dying trees common in older forest stands.

Another structural function of old-growth forests is related to nitrogen fixation. The microclimate created by a forest dominated by older trees, with their large branches, sustains many species of lichens that are known

Summer Wuerthner by old-growth Douglas fir along Frying Pan Creek.

as nitrogen fixers. These lichens take nitrogen from the atmosphere and fix, or chemically bind, it so that it's available to other plants for growth. Rain falling through these lichens removes this nitrogen and transports it to the soil, or the lichens themselves may fall to the ground, where they are incorporated in the forest litter and eventually contribute to soil nutrient enhancement. These lichens add about two to five pounds of nitrogen per acre annually. Such lichens are uncommon in younger forests, particularly those managed for timber production.

The large branches of these forest giants create their own environment for many specialized species of plants and animals. The branches support ferns, mosses, and lichens that provide food and habitat for other animals. More than 1,500 species of insects depend upon the forest canopy for their homes.

Older forests are dominated by downed woody debris, which a non-scientist might view simply as dead logs lying on the ground. In a typical old-growth Douglas fir forest, a tree falls every two years, and half of the annual litter fall is woody debris.

These fallen logs benefit the forest in several ways. If a forest fire burns through the stand, at least a portion of the large, often water-saturated downed logs typically remains unconsumed by the blaze and provides long-term sources of nutrients for forest regrowth. Additionally, they may create a natural fire break and stall the spread of a forest fire. Also, nitrogen-fixing bacteria are more abundant in old downed logs than in the soil, adding valuable nitrogen to the ecosystem. Since managed forests tend to have few large logs and little downed woody debris, timber production results in a slow decline in forest productivity over time.

The decaying logs also help perpetuate the forest. In the severe competition for space among living plants on the forest floor, tree seedlings have a difficult time germinating and surviving long enough to establish root systems. Moist fallen logs provide germination sites for seedlings as well as a source of moisture during the summer drought. Such logs are called "nurse" logs. Long colonnades of trees that all sprouted on the same fallen nurse log are a common sight in the lower-elevation forests of the park.

In the Pacific Northwest, it takes 500 to 600 years for a large fallen log to be 90 percent decomposed. Due to the slow rate of decomposition, coupled with the huge annual production of biomass, the accumulation of downed woody debris probably exceeds decomposition, and subsequent

Old-growth forest along Tahoma Creek. Down woody debris and snags are critical structural components of the old growth forest, providing habitat for many different species.

nutrient uptake by roots, until a stand exceeds a thousand years of age, at which point a steady-state balance is sometimes achieved. Studies in the Olympics and Western Cascades have found that 10 to 20 percent of the forest floor is covered by fallen logs. In Mount Rainier as much as 150 tons of woody debris per acre has been measured. For decades, foresters mistakenly considered such dead material as wasted resources. From an ecological perspective, however, dead trees and snags are not wasted.

Snags are critical habitat for many other wildlife species. Insects, fungi, and bacteria use these snags, which also provide homes for cavity-nesting birds, mammals, reptiles, and amphibians, including flying squirrels, bats, wood ducks and goldeneyes, nuthatches, woodpeckers, and chickadees. The large snags found in natural forests provide more potential nesting sites than do the small trees found in managed forests. When snags fall onto the ground, many animals, from salamanders to voles, find shelter under the downed logs.

Some snags fall into streams and rivers, where they serve different, but critical, structural and nutrient cycling purposes. Cold water inhibits the decomposition of logs, and in a typical small stream flowing through an old-growth forest, these logs are long-term structural resources for many species of aquatic insects and other invertebrates, which live in or upon the logs. They also provide the structural habitat critical for fish, including salmon and trout. Studies have shown that 50 percent of the salmon and trout habitat in smaller streams is produced by fallen logs.

In addition, logs in streams create a stair-step structure of pools and small falls that helps protect banks from erosion. The falling water also traps oxygen, helping to aerate streams, providing the oxygen so critical for the survival of fish and other organisms. Logs also trap sediment.

Natural Disturbances

Natural agents of disturbance include floods, avalanches, windstorms, volcanic eruptions, mudflows, and wildfires. The most important disturbance that controls species distribution within Mount Rainier National Park is wildfire. Wildfire, rather than being destructive, is a creative force. Before the days of effective fire suppression, wildfires were common and normal in the region. Wildfire has been documented on over 90 percent of the forest stands within Mount Rainier. There were frequent references to smoke and fire by many of the early expeditions to the mountain. For instance, near Bear Prairie just south of the Nisqually River, Hazard Stevens, the first to successfully climb Mount Rainier in 1870, noted that "the whole region had been swept by fire: thousands of giant trunks stood blackened and lifeless. . . ." Later Stevens notes that "the country was much obscured with smoke from heavy fires which had been raging on the Cowlitz the last two days."

In 1883, another climbing party that included George Bayley and P. B. Van Trump traveled to Mount Rainier and noted that "the woods were on fire around us, and we occasionally found ourselves hemmed in by flame and blinding smoke; smoldering trunks lay across the trail and half-burned stumps left treacherous pitfalls in our way." Later during the climb, Bayley remarked that "the pall of dense smoke that had overhung the whole country for two months lifted for a few moments . . . giving us our first inspiring view of Mount Tacoma. . . ." And George Dickson, another climber, wrote in 1892 that "I found the forest fires had done much damage since I was here the year before." What is astounding about these early references is that nearly every party that visited Rainier in the early years commented about the presence of smoke and fires, or witnessed ongoing fires or the aftermath of past fires.

Fourteen major fires have occurred within the park since a 1230 A.D. blaze that affected 47 percent of the park's forested stands. Other significant fires burned in 1303, 1403, 1503, 1628, 1688, 1703, 1803, 1825, 1856, 1858, 1872, 1886, and 1934. Most larger burns are associated with periodic severe drought.

Large or small, fires don't usually kill all trees. Fires create a mosaic of charred, slightly charred, and unburned stands. The burn pattern is influenced by wind, age and structure of the existing forest, and other factors. When a tree is burned, but not killed, a fire scar results. The wound often heals over. Scientists can reconstruct past fire frequency and history by reviewing the fire scars from many trees over a drainage. Analysis of Mount Rainier's forests shows the average fire interval prior to European settlement was approximately 465 years. The interval dropped to 226 years in the 1800s. Whether this is due to more human ignited fires, more arid climatic conditions at the end of the Little Ice Age, or both is unknown. Nevertheless, the correlation between drought periods and large fires is remarkably close. When severe drought conditions exist, it's essentially impossible to suppress a fire, even with our modern firefighting equipment. Such severe fire conditions are infrequent, and we tend to view them as catastrophic when, in fact, they are quite normal. Disturbances like fires are not disasters, but an important part of a functioning forest ecosystem. They recycle nutrients, cleanse the forest of pathogens, and create snags and other valuable woody debris critical to the survival of many other species. It's not fires that endanger forests, but fire suppression.

Most of the park's forests originated from one large fire or another. The large, old-growth 750-year-old trees in the Ohanapecosh River drainage sprouted in the aftermath of the 1230 fire. Most of Mount Rainier's extensive 350-year-old trees dominating the upper Carbon, Puyallup, Mowich, and Nisqually drainages originated in a fire in 1628. Many of the trees in the White River drainage owe their origins to a big fire in 1703.

Not every part of the park is equally susceptible to blazes, even in a severe fire year. Moist locations, like north-facing slopes and valley bottoms, as well as areas with limited fuels, like rocky ridges, all experience

Snags from a wildfire. Wildfire is a rejuvenating natural process that shapes and influences nearly all plant communities in the park.

far fewer fires, and most of the really ancient trees in the park grow in such locations. For example, the old-growth Grove of the Patriarchs is located on an island in the Ohanapecosh River where the trees are protected from most blazes.

Some of Mount Rainier's plant species are adapted to periodic fire. Douglas fir requires abundant sunlight for successful regeneration and almost always germinates after a major fire. Large Douglas firs have trunks that are free of lower branches that might carry a fire up into the canopy. They also have extremely thick bark that provides adequate protection against all but the most severe fires. Western white pine is another fire-dependent species, typically germinating after fires. Vine maple and beargrass sprout from rootstocks after a fire, ensuring their regeneration on fire-dominated sites. Not surprisingly, all these species are more abundant on the drier eastern side of Mount Rainier, where fires are more common.

Avalanches affect 7 percent of the forested areas of the park. Most of the avalanche tracks are located in the White and Cowlitz drainages. Interestingly, most large avalanche chutes are associated with past burns. The fires remove the forest and create conditions that foster snowslides, which continue to keep the pathways open.

Working over longer time intervals, the advance and retreat of glaciers, mudflows, and volcanic eruptions all create opportunities for new plant growth. These disturbances are less regular than fires or avalanches. On a smaller scale, wind-thrown trees also create small forest openings. All of these disturbances, along with physical attributes like slope, temperature, and precipitation, contribute to the intricate mosaic of plant community types and habitats encountered in the park today.

Despite all these occurrences, there are parts of Mount Rainier that haven't experienced a major disturbance in more than 1,000 years. These areas include Cougar Creek Campground, Upper Cowlitz drainage, Cataract Creek, Ipsut Creek, and the confluence of Chinook Creek and Ohanapecosh River.

Species Accounts

Coniferous Trees

SITKA SPRUCE
(Picea sitchensis)

Description. Light green needles stiff and sharp, up to an inch in length, projecting outward on all sides of the twig. If you grab the branch and it hurts, it's probably a spruce. Needles are four-sided and can be rolled in the fingers. Cones 2 to 3 inches long, with thin, papery, irregularly toothed scales. Scaly, purplish brown bark. Base of mature tree trunks often buttressed. Trunks very straight, with little taper, reaching nearly 300 feet in height and 10 feet or more in diameter.
Distribution. Rare in the park; limited to the rain forest along the lower Carbon River Valley.
Remarks. Sitka spruce is a coastal species seldom found far from the ocean strand. Its occurrence at Mount Rainier is unusual. Sitka spruce is named after Sitka, Alaska, where the tree is extremely common. The species is the fourth tallest tree in the world and is common in the cool, wet coastal belt from northern California to Alaska's Kodiak Island.

GRAND FIR
(Abies grandis)

Description. Needles are broad, ¾ to 2 inches, spreading in a flat plane from twig like teeth on a comb. Tips of needles often notched. Dark green above, with two distinct white stomatal stripes below. Cones are cylindrical, 2 to 4 inches, greenish, and borne erect on tips of branches. Bark is gray to light brown; smooth and resin-blistered when young but becomes more furrowed with age. Reaches 200 feet in height and 5 feet in diameter.

Distribution. Mixed with other conifers in lower-elevation forests, particularly in the Nisqually and White River drainages.

Remarks. Tends to be found in drier forests, hence more common east of the Cascades. Most abundant in the White River Valley, in the rain shadow of Mount Rainier.

DOUGLAS FIR
(Pseudotsuga menziesii)

Description. Blunt-pointed needles ½ to 1½ inches radiating around the twig. Light brown (green when immature) cones 2 to 4 inches with three-pronged "rat's tails" sticking out from under thin scales. Bark light gray and smooth in young trees, becoming corky, deeply furrowed, thick, and brown with age. Height nearly 300 feet, with diameters of 14 feet. Broad, rounded crown; long, branch-free lower trunks in mature trees.

Distribution. One of the most widely distributed trees in the Pacific Northwest; found throughout the park at low to mid elevations. Common in Ohanapecosh and Cowlitz River Valleys.

Remarks. *Pseudotsuga* means "false hemlock"; however it is not a hemlock, nor is it a fir. It is named for botanist David Douglas, who collected its seeds while on an expedition to the Pacific Northwest in 1825. The common giant of the old-growth forest, Douglas fir can live over 1,000 years. Its thick bark makes it highly resistant to fire. Intolerant of deep shade, the seedlings often establish themselves on sites after fires. Old-growth Douglas fir is scattered throughout the park but can best be seen at the Grove of the Patriarchs and in the Carbon River Valley.

WESTERN HEMLOCK
(Tsuga heterophylla)

Description. Soft, light green needles with white stomatal stripes beneath, spread in delicate, flat sprays, from ¼ to ¾ inch. Cones oblong, ¾ to 1 inch, hanging from branch tips. Cones are purplish green when young, turning brown when mature. Gray bark, thick and furrowed in mature trees. Top leader of tree conspicuously drooped; lower branches bend gracefully downward. Height to 200 feet.

Distribution. The dominant tree in the low-elevation forests of the park, typically found between 1,700 and 3,300 feet.

Remarks. Highly shade tolerant. Most common understory species in mature forests, where it eventually replaces other species such as Douglas fir and western red cedar in climax forests. Browsed heavily by elk in winter.

MOUNTAIN HEMLOCK
(Tsuga mertensiana)

Description. Needles ½ to ¾ inch. Bluish green with white stomatal stripes on top and bottom. Needles radiate from all sides of the twig. Cones 1 to 2½ inches, usually larger than those of western hemlock; borne on upper branch tips, often purplish on immature trees, turning brown with age. Bark dark brown and furrowed. Mature crown rather broad, with drooping branches that sweep upward toward the tips. Height to 100 feet.

Distribution. Subalpine up to timberline throughout the park, often growing in forest islands among subalpine meadows.

Remarks. A timberline species from California's Sierra Nevada north to Alaska. Typically grows in wet, snowy environments. Its flexible branches can sustain heavy snow loads without breakage. Summer drought limits growth. Trees often reach 500 to 700 years of age.

WESTERN RED CEDAR
(Thuja plicata)

Description. Scalelike needles in opposite pairs tightly pressed against the twigs. Has one pair of folded needles and second pair of nonfolded needles. Branches are flattened and appear limp, with an upward turn at the tips. Bark is light gray and can be ripped off in long, fibrous strips. Cones ½ inch in open clusters. Will reach heights of 200 feet with diameters of up to 20 feet.

Distribution. Moist soils. Common in low-elevation forest throughout the park. Some of the larger trees in the Grove of the Patriarchs are western red cedar. Large cedars are also found along the Carbon River, Nisqually River, Tahoma Creek, Mowich River, and other locations in the park.

Remarks. This rot-resistant tree was used by Native Americans for a variety of purposes. The wood is soft and easily worked, making it ideal for totem poles and canoes. The wood splits easily into flat sheets and was used for house construction. Early white settlers often made roofs of cedar shakes.

ALASKA YELLOW CEDAR
(Chamaecyparis nootkatensis)

Description. Scalelike, blue-green needles encase the twig, which is slightly wider than thick. Unlike western red cedar, which has two rows of folded and two rows of nonfolded leaves, in Alaska yellow cedar, all four rows of scalelike leaves have the same appearance. Needles prickly to touch. Flattened branches appear limp and hang vertically. Berry-like, ½-inch cones ripen to brownish, mushroom-shaped scales. Bark grayish strips. Height up to 130 feet.

Distribution. Moist soils. Typically above 3,000 feet in avalanche chutes, rocky areas, and ridgelines in the subalpine zone up to timberline, sometimes even mixed

Alaska yellow cedar bough.

among Pacific silver fir. Grows where the melting of snowpack produces cold, wet soils.

Remarks. A slow-growing, long-lived tree, with older individuals surviving more than 1,000 years. The park's oldest trees are Alaska cedar over 1,200 years old growing in the Ipsut Creek Valley. This shade-tolerant tree often starts in the understory of other species and lives so long it becomes a rare climax species.

WHITEBARK PINE
(Pinus albicaulis)

Description. Needles 1 to 3 inches long occurring in groups of five. Egg-shaped cones are purple when immature, turning brownish when mature. Bark is thin, scaly, and grayish white. The trunk is typically multistemmed with a broad, airy crown.

Distribution. Rare in the park; primarily found on dry, rocky areas near timberline. A good place to see this species is on rocky ridges above Sunrise.

Remarks. The seeds of whitebark pine are large and nutritious. Bears, squirrels, and even some birds such as the Clark's nutcracker collect and eat the seeds. Whitebark pine's open crown permits wind to sweep away heavy snow, reducing breakage of branches.

Whitebark pine is rare in the park, but can be found in the White River drainage.

WESTERN WHITE PINE
(Pinus monticola)

Description. A lovely tall pine with a straight, tapering bole free of branches for one-third of the trunk in mature individuals. Needles blue-green, 2 to 4 inches long, in clusters of five. Cones thin and linear, 6 to 10 inches in length, borne on tips of upper branches. Bark gray and cracking into squares in older individuals.
Distribution. Widely scattered, often only a minor component of the forest. More common on the eastern side of the park. Tends to grow at mid elevations, often recolonizing areas after a fire.
Remarks. An introduced disease, white pine blister rust, is causing white pine to die out in much of the West. Genetically resistant white pine is being bred and used to restock parts of the West, but it will be centuries before these trees can grow large enough to replace the majestic tall pines that are dying off.

LODGEPOLE PINE
(Pinus contorta)

Description. Yellow-green needles 1 to 2½ inches long, in sets of two. Egg-shaped cones up to 2 inches long will persist on trees for years, with even young trees less than ten years of age bearing cones. Bark is thin and scaly, reddish brown to gray.
Distribution. Rare in the park; found on drier rubble at 4,500 feet in the White River Valley. Look for it near the terminus of the Emmons Glacier.
Remarks. One of the most adaptable trees, growing in nutrient-deficient, boggy soils along the coast as well as in dry, cold environments near timberline. The straight-growing Rocky Mountain form is found at Rainier. The straight trunks with limited taper were used by the Plains Indians for tepee lodge poles, giving rise to the tree's common name.

PONDEROSA PINE
(Pinus ponderosa)

Description. Needles 4 to 10 inches long, in groups of three. Roundish, 3- to 5-inch cones reddish when immature, brown when mature; scales have recurved barbs on tips. Bark thick, reddish yellow with scales like jigsaw puzzle pieces. Tall, branch-free lower bole on mature individuals.

Distribution. Rare in the park; found primarily on the eastern fringe.

Remarks. Very common on the eastern slopes of the Cascades, where it is extremely tolerant to low-intensity fires. In areas where natural fires have been allowed to occur, these trees grow in open, parklike stands. Such open forests are extremely rare, however, as policies of fire suppression and overgrazing by livestock have caused thickets of young ponderosa pines to develop in most of its range.

WESTERN YEW
(Taxus brevifolia)

Description. Small to medium-size tree. Needles green above and pale below, with soft points and short stalks where they are attached to twigs. Instead of cones, yews produce a red, berrylike fruit. Bark thin, scaly, and reddish. Branching is crooked.

Distribution. Grows as understory tree in moist lowland forests. Occurs widely but seldom abundant; typically 1 to 5 percent of the understory cover.

Remarks. Grows so slowly that a 10-inch-diameter tree may be 300 to 700 years old. This tree was once considered a trash species that got in the way of logging more valuable species. The yew gained new respect in the early 1990s, when a substance produced by the bark, known as taxol, began being used to treat cancer.

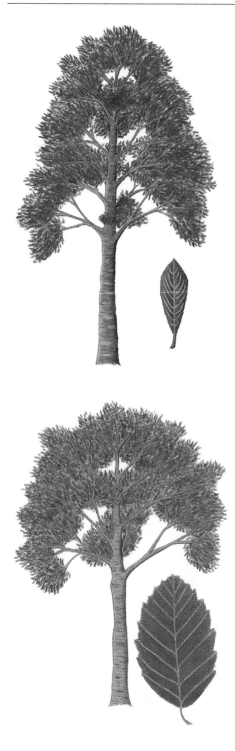

BITTER CHERRY
(Prunus emarginata)

Description. A smallish tree up to 80 feet, usually less. Alternate leaves 1 to 3 inches long, oblong to oval, finely toothed, and rounded at the tip. The 1/2-inch flowers are white, with twenty to thirty yellow stamens in the center, and borne in loose clusters. Cherries are 1/2 inch and reddish. Bark reddish brown with horizontal rows of pores.
Distribution. Low elevations along streams or in recently logged areas.
Remarks. Cherries are so sour they are inedible. Birds, however, love the fruit.

RED ALDER
(Alnus ruba)

Description. A fast-growing tree that may reach heights of 100 feet. Looks something like the white-barked paper birch of the North Woods. Leaves are opposite, oval, coarsely toothed, and 3 to 4 inches. Male and female catkins appear on the same tree. Female catkins are conelike, small, and brown. Bark is smooth and often covered with light-colored lichens.
Distribution. Gravel bars and river terraces. Forms open, airy glades.
Remarks. Often invades recently logged land (logging doesn't occur in the park) and other disturbed sites such as recently burned areas. Roots host bacteria that convert atmospheric nitrogen into a form available to other plants and are critical to soil development.

Red alder along Ohanapecosh River.

Shrubs to Small Trees

DOUGLAS MAPLE
(Acer glabrum douglasii)

Description. Small tree or shrub, some-times reaching 35 feet in height. Oppo-site, toothed, maplelike leaves with three to five lobes. Red-orange in fall. V-shaped winged seeds, seldom over 1 inch. Bark light gray.

Distribution. Dry ridges to well-drained seep sites. Usually found in drier, sunnier sites than vine maple.

Remarks. Related to Rocky Mountain maple, a favorite food of elk, deer, and other species. Named for botanist David Douglas.

VINE MAPLE
(Acer circinatum)

Description. Green, multistemmed shrub or small tree up to 20 feet tall. Opposite, toothed leaves with seven to nine lobes; turn red to yellow in autumn. Winged seeds form straight line rather than V shape.

Distribution. One of the most common understory shrubs in the park.

Remarks. A favorite food of elk and deer. One reason the shrub is so successful is that it has three different means of reproduction: It produces good crops of seeds, which are scattered by the wind. If the aboveground parts are clipped or destroyed, as in a fire, the tree can sprout from root crowns. And if a branch is put in contact with the ground, such as by heavy snow, the branch will develop its own root system.

Vine maple, a common understory tree of the forest.

SITKA ALDER
(Alnus sinuata)

Description. Shrub to small tree up to 20 feet tall. Multiple branches from root crown. Leaves 1 to 4 inches, oval, with pointed tips and double-toothed margins. Male and female catkins appear on the same shrub. Female catkins are ½ inch long, oblong, and conelike. Bark grayish.
Distribution. Common on avalanche chutes and along mountain streams. Grows from lowlands to subalpine basins.
Remarks. Named for Sitka, Alaska, where it is abundant. Like red alder, Sitka alder has root bacteria able to fix atmospheric nitrogen, making it available for other plant growth.

COMMON CHOKECHERRY
(Prunus virginiana)

Description. Small tree to 20 feet, but typically less. Leaves are 2 to 4 inches, oval, with fine-toothed margins. White flowers ⅜ inch, borne in long racemes or clusters. Edible black fruit.
Distribution. Common in disturbed sites and sunny forest openings.
Remarks. Fruit makes excellent jellies and syrup and is relished by bears, birds, and other wildlife.

WESTERN SERVICEBERRY
(Amelanchier alnifolia)

Description. Shrub to small tree up to 15 feet. Smooth, gray bark. Alternate, round-oval leaves with teeth on the upper half. Flowers white. Fruit dull red, turning purple-black; looks something like a blueberry.
Distribution. Forest edges, rocky talus slopes, and other openings.
Remarks. Fruit is edible, if not tasty. Wildlife loves this plant. The berries are relished by black bear and birds; elk and deer browse the branches in winter.

DEVIL'S CLUB
(Oplopanax horridus)

Description. Erect, thick, untapering stem armed with numerous spines. Large, maple-shaped leaves also have spines on the undersides. Whitish green flowers in compact terminal clusters. Clusters of bright red berries.

Distribution. Moist woods along streams and seepage areas, as well as avalanche chutes. One of the most common understory plants in the lowland western hemlock forests.

Remarks. The aptly named devil's club often forms dense thickets that are difficult to move through. The spines contain a mild toxin and can cause swelling.

Devil's club.

WHITE RHODODENDRON
(Rhododendron albiflorum)

Description. Erect shrub up to 8 feet tall. Young twigs covered with coarse, reddish hairs. Yellowish green leaves with rusty hairs on upper surface. Leaves are alternate in clusters on branch. Large, showy, creamy-white flowers grow in clusters of two to four. Fruit a dry capsule.
Distribution. Mostly found in subalpine meadows along the edge of tree clumps and on well-drained sites.
Remarks. The terminal cluster of leaves looks something like fool's huckleberry.

NOOTKA ROSE
(Rosa nutkana)

Description. Spindly shrub to 10 feet tall. Two large prickles at the base of each leaf, but seldom any other spines on plant. Compound leaves with odd numbers of toothed leaflets. Large, solitary, pink flowers typically borne at branch tips. Fruit reddish, round, berrylike rose hips.
Distribution. Open habitat along meadows, streamsides, and clearings.
Remarks. Rose hips are high in vitamin C and were often consumed by Native Americans.

WESTERN THIMBLEBERRY
(Rubus parviflorus)

Description. Forms dense thickets. Looks something like devil's club but without spines. Large, maple-shaped leaves with four to seven lobes. Large, white flowers with yellow centers. Domed, raspberry-like, bright red berries.
Distribution. Open sites in avalanche chutes, on roadsides, and along edges of trails at low to mid elevations.
Remarks. Berries are sweet and edible.

SALMONBERRY
(Rubus spectabilis)

Description. Erect shrub, often forming dense thickets. Leaves dark green and sharply toothed, typically lobed into three leaflets. Large, red-pink flowers. Raspberrylike yellow or reddish fruit. Scattered prickles here and there on brown stems.
Distribution. Moist to wet places along streams, avalanche chutes, and roadsides.
Remarks. Forms extensive clones. Berries are edible; taste varies among clones.

RED ELDERBERRY
(Sambucus racemosa)

Description. Shrub to small tree up to 18 feet. Soft pithy twigs. Leaves opposite and divided in large, lance-shaped, sharply toothed leaflets. White flowers in terminal clusters. Fruits bright red, berrylike drupes.
Distribution. Streambanks and other moist areas at low to mid elevations.
Remarks. Bears love the berries, and a tasty jelly can be made from them.

Red elderberry.

SITKA MOUNTAIN ASH
(Sorbus sitchensis)

Description. Small, erect tree with several stems. Leaves are alternate, divided into seven to eleven leaflets, with toothed margins and rounded tips. White flowers in round-topped terminal clusters. Bright, orange-red berries in terminal clusters.
Distribution. Openings such as the edge of parklands at mid to high elevations.
Remarks. The berries are a favorite with birds, particularly in the winter. Cascades mountain ash *(Sorbus scopulina)* is very similar, but with narrower leaflets that are pointed at the tip.

RED HUCKLEBERRY
(Vaccinium parvifolium)

Description. Erect shrub to 12 feet, with very strongly angled, bright green branches. Alternate, oval leaves not toothed. Yellowish green or pinkish bell- or urn-shaped flowers. Bright red, round berries.

Distribution. Associated with decaying wood, growing on stumps or fallen logs. Often grows under forest canopy.

Remarks. Fruit is edible but sparse.

THIN-LEAVED HUCKLEBERRY
(Vaccinium membranaceum)

Description. Alternate, lance-shaped to elliptic leaves with pointed tips and finely toothed margin. Turn red in fall. Urn-shaped, creamy pink to yellow-pink flowers. Black to purplish fruit.

Distribution. Dry forests and open sites, particularly in old burns.

Remarks. One of the best-tasting huckleberries. Very abundant on open burned hillsides. Now less common than in the past, due to fire suppression.

OCEANSPRAY
(Holodiscus discolor)

Description. Shrub up to 12 feet tall. Leaves are alternate, triangular, and coarsely toothed. Small, white to cream flowers in lilaclike terminal clusters that turn brown and remain on plant over winter.

Distribution. Open sites at low to mid elevations.

Remarks. Very hard wood, sometimes called ironwood. Used by Indians as digging sticks.

Ferns

Ferns, unlike flowering plants, do not produce seeds; rather, they release spores. The position of sori, where the spores are produced, and the nature of their indusium, or covering, are critical to positive identification, although some ferns can be identified based on physical appearance. Twenty-three species of ferns have been reported for Mount Rainier. The following are among the most common.

MAIDENHAIR FERN
(*Adiantum pedatum*)

Description. Forms delicate, palmately branched, fan-shaped clumps. Leaves have dark brown to black stems. Oblong leaflets.
Distribution. Shady, moist sites on cliffs; spray zone around waterfalls; and seeps.
Remarks. Often forms dense colonies.

LADY FERN
(*Athyrium filix-femina*)

Description. Fronds clustered, up to 6 feet long, and spreading. Lance-shaped leaves, narrow toward both ends. Twice or thrice compound leaves.
Distribution. Moist forests and streambanks.
Remarks. Native Americans used the leaves to cover food.

DEER FERN
(*Blechnum spicant*)

Description. Evergreen, tufted fern that forms clumps. Looks something like a small sword fern, except the leaflets are attached to the leaf axis along their bases. Two kinds of fronds: sterile ones, which are clustered about the fertile centerpiece and frequently pressed to the ground, and spore-bearing leaves, which are taller and stand at the center of each clump.
Distribution. Moist forests and streambanks.
Remarks. An important winter food for deer and elk.

Flowers

The park is home to more than 700 species of flowers. Listed here are some of the more abundant and showy flowers you are likely to encounter.

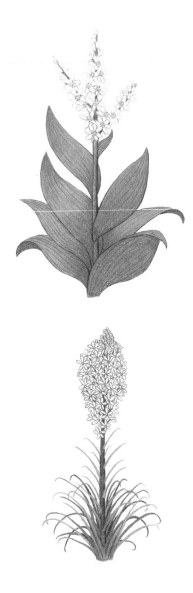

White Flowers

FALSE HELLEBORE
(Veratrum californicum)

Description. Greenish white flowers borne in terminal panicles. Oval leaves 8 to 12 inches long, with prominent veins. Height to 5 feet.
Distribution. Wet meadows from lowlands to subalpine. Usually grows in dense clumps.
Remarks. False hellebore contains alkaloids that are fatal if eaten in large doses.

BEARGRASS
(Xerophyllum tenax)

Description. One of the showiest flowers in the park. What appears to be one conspicuous large, white flower actually consists of hundreds of small, white blossoms in a dense, conical raceme. Flowering stalk is 3 feet tall and grows from a basal clump of sharp-edged, grasslike leaves. Often entire slopes are covered with these flowers.
Distribution. Open woods, mountain slopes. Most abundant at mid elevations.
Remarks. Very resistant to fire and quickly sprouts from root crown after a fire. Does not flower each year, thus some years are better than others for blooms.

False hellebore.

COW PARSNIP
(Heracleum lanatum)

Description. A large, conspicuous, coarse, hairy plant growing to 7 feet tall. White flowers in flat-topped umbel as much as 1 foot across. Leaves composed of three leaflets up to 12 inches across, coarsely toothed, and palmately lobed in shape. Hollow stem.

Distribution. Damp soils, particularly along streams, in avalanche chutes, and in open woods.

Remarks. Elk and black bear eat the stalks.

Avalanche lily.

TRILLIUM
(Trillium ovatum)

Description. Showy white flowers that turn pinkish with age on terminal stalks. Three white petals and three green sepals. Leaves in whorls of three and somewhat triangular in shape. Often blooms in May.

Distribution. Moist woodlands at low to mid elevations.

Remarks. The major dispersal mechanism for trillium seeds is ants, which carry the seeds back to their nests, eat an oily appendage found on each seed, and then discard the seed.

VANILLALEAF
(Achlys triphylla)

Description. Small white flowers that lack sepals and petals, in showy white spikes that stick up above the leaves. Three fan-shaped, blunt-toothed leaflets held nearly horizontal.

Distribution. Moist, shady forests, low to mid elevations. Often creates a continuous carpet of green leaves on the forest floor.

Remarks. Plant has vanillalike fragrance when dry.

Vanillaleaf.

Mountain pasqueflower.

WESTERN ANEMONE
(Anemone occidentalis)

Description. Very hairy stem and leaves. Leaves divided into narrow segments. Large, white flowers sometimes tinged with blue. Distinctive featherlike seedpod looks like the hairy head of a sheepdog.
Distribution. Subalpine and alpine meadows.
Remarks. Also known as pasqueflower. Blooms as soon as snow melts. The hairy seedpods dotting meadows in afternoon light look like hundreds of tiny lightbulbs ablaze.

TOLMIE'S SAXIFRAGE
(Saxifraga tolmiei)

Description. Low, mat-forming plant with tiny, fleshy, club-shaped leaves. Saucer-shaped flowers with distinctly separated white petals.
Distribution. Rocky slopes, cliffs, near snowbeds in alpine locations.
Remarks. Named for Dr. William Tolmie, botanical collector and a physician at the Hudson's Bay Fort Nisqually, and the first white to attempt to climb Mount Rainier.

SITKA VALERIAN
(Valeriana sitchensis)

Description. Small, white flowers with sweet scent. Stamens protrude from dense terminal cluster of flowers. Leaves opposite, divided into three to seven coarsely toothed leaflets.
Distribution. Moist subalpine meadows.
Remarks. Valerian was used in Europe as an aphrodisiac.

MARSH MARIGOLD
(Clatha biflora)

Description. Heart-shaped, blunt-toothed leaves. Showy white flowers, with two on a stem.
Distribution. Seepage sites in subalpine areas.
Remarks. One of the first flowers to appear from under snow banks.

Pink or Red Flowers

COLUMBINE
(Aquilegia formosa)

Description. Red and yellow flowers with red spurs and protruding styles. Mostly basal leaves, twice divided in five-lobed blades.
Distribution. Moist, open to partly shady sites, including meadows, forest glades, and avalanche chutes.
Remarks. Very attractive to hummingbirds.

PINK MOUNTAIN HEATHER
(Phyllodoce empetriformis)

Description. Low, much branched, matlike plant with erect evergreen stems. Alternate, needlelike, linear leaves with groove on lower surface. Showy, bell-shaped, pink to rose flowers in terminal clusters.
Distribution. Subalpine meadows and parks.
Remarks. There are several similar-looking species of mountain heather. Yellow mountain heather (Phyllodoce glanduliflora) is found near timberline, white-flowered heather (C. mertensiana) in subalpine locations, and white-flowered Alaskan heather (C. stelleriana) at lower elevations.

Red monkey flower is common along streams in subalpine parks.

MONKEY FLOWER
(Mimulus lewisii)

Description. Showy, red to pink trumpet-shaped flowers, strongly two-lipped, the lower lips marked with yellow. Large, conspicuously veined leaves clasping to stem in pairs.

Distribution. Along cold streams and seeps at mid elevations.

Remarks. Named for Meriwether Lewis of the Lewis and Clark Expedition.

Red paintbrush and lousewort.

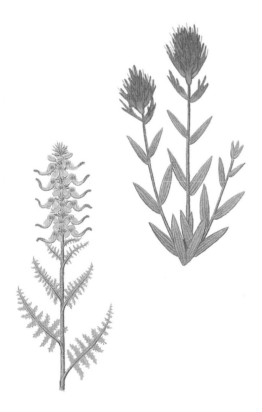

SCARLET INDIAN PAINTBRUSH
(Castilleja miniata)

Description. Pointed reddish bracts (which look like they are the flowers) cover the actual flowers, which are greenish and tubular. Linear to lance-shaped leaves, sometimes with shallow lobes.
Distribution. Open woods and meadows.
Remarks. Partially parasitic, tapping into the roots of other plants for a portion of their food.

ELEPHANTHEAD
(Pedicularis groenlandica)

Description. Purplish pink, beaked flower that resembles the head and trunk of an elephant. Basal leaves fernlike and finely divided.
Distribution. Wet meadows at mid elevations.
Remarks. Common throughout the Cascades, Rockies, and up to Alaska.

MOSS CAMPION
(Silene acaulis)

Description. Showy, pink, stalkless flowers on a green, mosslike bed of short, linear, lance-shaped basal leaves.
Distribution. Well-drained but moist alpine sites.
Remarks. A cushion plant adapted to harsh alpine conditions. Low plant profile helps to avoid abrasion from wind and raises internal temperature of plant, thereby increasing photosynthesis.

Yellow Flowers

GLACIER LILY
(Erythronium grandiflorum)

Description. One to two yellow flowers per stem, each with six reflexed tepals (like sepals). Elliptic basal leaves 4 to 6 inches long. Plant 6 to 12 inches tall.
Distribution. Damp subalpine meadows, blooming just after snow patches disappear.
Remarks. The bulbs of this plant are edible and are a favorite of bears.

SKUNK CABBAGE
(Lysichitum americanum)

Description. Basal rosette of lance-shaped leaves up to 4 feet long. Flowers yellow on a spike, hooded by a bright yellow bract.
Distribution. Swamps, seepage areas in low-elevation forests.
Remarks. Robust plant with leaves so large it looks almost tropical.

YELLOW MONKEY FLOWER
(*Mimulus guttatus*)

Description. Large, yellow, two-lipped, trumpet-shaped flower. Oval leaves, coarsely toothed, in pairs clasping to stem. Plant up to 2 feet tall.

Distribution. Wet seeps, along streams and springs.

Remarks. Native Americans used the leaves for greens, eating them fresh like lettuce.

Lupine.

Purple or Blue Flowers

LUPINE
(Lupinus latifolius)

Description. Blue-purple flowers in long, dense racemes. Leaves palmate with seven to nine leaflets 1 to 2 inches long. Stems branched.
Distribution. Open meadows.
Remarks. Lupine often forms thick beds of blossoms.

BLUEBELLS
(Mertensia paniculata)

Description. Bell-shaped blue flowers with slight pink cast, in open cluster dropping from top of stem. Heart-shaped leaves with distinct veins.
Distribution. Moist to wet meadows and open forests.
Remarks. Elk, pikas, and marmots all consume bluebells.

its own home stream, affecting such things as the timing of runs and the downstream migration of fingerlings. Replacement with hatchery fish "pollutes" the gene pool of the wild fish. Furthermore, the hatchery fish are not as strong as wild fish, making them more vulnerable to habitat changes and more likely to contract diseases, which can spread through populations of both wild and hatchery fish. Biologists believe the only way to save salmon in the Pacific Northwest is to save the wild fish stocks and their habitat. Unfortunately, dams on many of the rivers originating within Mount Rainier National Park have substantially reduced or eliminated salmon runs. Restoration can occur only if downstream dams are removed.

Mount Rainier's native fish include rainbow trout, coastal cutthrout trout, Dolly Varden/bull trout, mountain whitefish, and one or more sculpin species. Salmon historically native to park rivers include coho, chinook, and steelhead or sea-run rainbow. Sockeye and chum salmon may have occurred in park streams, but their exact status is unknown.

Salmon spawning runs in the Cowlitz and Ohanapecosh Rivers are blocked by dams at Mayfield and Riffle Lakes. Coho are transported around these dams. Dams on the Puyallup-Mowish and the Nisqually prevent upstream passage of anadromous fish into the headwaters of these park streams. The Mud Mountain Dam on the White River creates a barrier to upstream fish passage; however, coho, chinook, and steelhead are all transported around the dam. The only park river without dams blocking fish passage is the Carbon, but a canyon eight miles downstream from the park partially blocks upstream migration. Below the dams, coho salmon still run up the White, Carbon, North and South Puyallup, and Mowich Rivers. Chinook salmon are found in the White and the West Fork of the White River. Steelhead are found in the Carbon River.

Because of impassable barriers such as falls, periodic glacial outburst floods, and low productivity, none of the park's lakes supported fish populations until they were stocked, beginning officially in 1918 (although unofficial stocking likely began earlier). Stocking of native fish like rainbow and cutthroat trout, plus non-native species like brook trout and brown trout, has substantially changed the aquatic ecosystems in these previously fishless lakes. Fish stocking was terminated in 1972; nevertheless, fish populations persist in many park lakes. Of the ninety-seven park water bodies with a surface area greater than one acre, forty-four have been stocked with trout and thirty-seven are thought to currently hold fish.

Species Accounts

CHINOOK SALMON (KING)
(Oncorhynchus tshawytscha)

Description. Largest of the Pacific salmon, may reach weights of 100 pounds or more. Unlike the other Pacific salmon, their body shape does not change much during spawning. Black gums at base of teeth. Numerous black spots on a blue-green back; tannish sides turning to white on belly. Black spots cover upper and lower tail. Skin color turns from bright silver during sea life to a dark brown, sometimes approaching black, the more time spent in fresh water. Male and female are very similar, except for the male's larger size.

Distribution. Favors large rivers. Chinook may be seen in upriver migrations almost any month of the year but are more abundant in spring and fall. Rivers with chinook runs include the White and the West Fork of the White, although it is uncertain if chinook ascend these rivers into the park.

Remarks. Mature chinook will spend three to seven years at sea. Most are four to five years old when they return to spawn and range in weight from 10 to 50 pounds. Chinook are not often easily seen on the spawning grounds, as they normally choose deeper spawning areas.

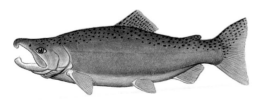

COHO SALMON (SILVER)
(Oncorhynchus kisutch)

Description. Male gets hooked jaw during spawning season. Black dots on upper part of back and upper half of tail only. Blue-green on back, shading to a white belly. At spawning time, the body becomes darker and the sides take on a reddish tinge. Gum area at base of teeth of lower jaw pale. Average 28 to 30 inches long, 6 to 10 pounds.

Distribution. Coho usually spawn in coastal rivers, sloughs, and side channels, entering streams in November and December. Coho runs persist in the Carbon, White, North and South Puyallup, and Mowich Rivers, although it is uncertain whether any Coho spawn in the park.

Remarks. Coho are sometimes known as blueback when caught before full maturity, and also as silvers. They are the most popular game fish of the salmon family and are one of the most valuable commercial species. Coho spend their first year in a river, making them more vulnerable than other salmon to habitat degradation. This is one reason they are endangered or threatened over much of their natural range south of Washington State. Typically return to spawn their third year.

SOCKEYE SALMON (RED)
(Oncorhynchus nerka)

Description. Color in spawning males bright red with green head. Males develop a hooked jaw and pronounced humped back.

Distribution. All sockeyes spawn only in river systems with a major lake. Mature four-year-old sockeyes average 6 pounds, and older age groups reach 12 pounds. Kokanee salmon, sockeyes that live year-round in lake systems, were planted in Alder Lake and run up the Nisqually River as far as the park.

Remarks. Juvenile sockeyes spend one to three years in a large lake before migrating to sea.

STEELHEAD OR RAINBOW TROUT
(Oncorhynchus mykiss)

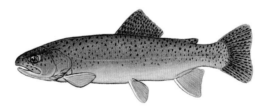

Description. Sea-run steelhead up to 45 inches long and 30 pounds; stream-dwelling rainbow trout much smaller. Usually bluish or greenish back, fading to silver-white on sides and belly. Distinctive red or pink lateral line down sides. Heavily spotted with black dots on back, sides, and tail.

Distribution. Steelhead are reported in the Carbon River, and rainbow trout have been planted in many park lakes.

Remarks. Rainbow trout and steelhead are the same fish—one a sea-run version of the other. As a result of genetic analysis, the steelhead/rainbow was recently determined to be a salmon, not a trout. Unlike other salmon, steelhead do not die after spawning and can return two to three times for spawning.

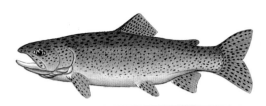

CUTTHROAT TROUT
(Oncorhynchus clarki)

Description. Bright red slash on either side of throat ("cut throat"); may be faint in fresh, sea-run fish. Dark greenish back, tannish sides, and white belly. Black spots cover tail, sides, and back. Although some subspecies can grow to 30 pounds or more, most usually not more than 1 to 4 pounds and 20 inches.
Distribution. Cutthroat trout live primarily in fresh water, including lakes. They have been stocked in many park lakes.
Remarks. The species name *clarki* refers to William Clark, coleader of the Lewis and Clark Expedition, who was the first to describe the species to science.

DOLLY VARDEN
(Salvelinus malma)

Description. Green-blue back fading to reddish belly. Sea-run fish very silvery. Moderately long head, no wormlike markings on back, and pink or red spots on sides. Anal and pelvic fins have white edges.
Distribution. Most of the major rivers draining the park are thought to hold native populations of bull trout, and recent surveys turned up bull trout specimens in the White, West Fork of the White, Carbon, and Puyallup Rivers.
Remarks. Until 1978, the Dolly Varden was divided into a coastal and interior form. Genetic analysis has determined that Dolly Varden trout are a separate species from the inland populations now called bull trout. The bull trout is threatened with extinction across much of its natural range and was recently listed as an endangered species. The coastal Dolly Varden is only slightly better off.

EASTERN BROOK TROUT
(Salvelinus fortinalis)

Description. Olive green back with wormlike markings. Red spots with blue halos on sides. Belly reddish, particularly in spawning fish. Maximum size is 14 pounds, but usually much smaller, less than a pound.
Distribution. Introduced fish, common in smaller creeks and some subalpine lakes.
Remarks. A fall spawner. Can be abundant in some lakes.

BROWN TROUT
(Salmo trutta)

Description. Under ideal conditions, can attain length of 3 feet and weight of 30 pounds. Fish in Rainier much smaller. Back and sides have reddish orange spots on yellowish brown background. Black spots on head. Belly white to yellowish cream.
Distribution. Planted in one of the Golden Lakes.
Remarks. Brown trout are native to Europe and widely distributed in North America. Considered more difficult to catch than native trout like cutthroat and rainbow.

MOUNTAIN WHITEFISH
(Prosopium williamsoni)

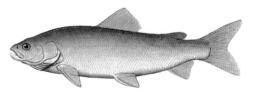

Description. Troutlike body up to a foot, sometimes larger. Mouth small with no teeth. Long, pointed snout. Generally silver color with darker brownish back.
Distribution. Exact distribution in park not known. Commonly found in lakes and streams.
Remarks. Primarily a bottom feeder, eating aquatic insects.

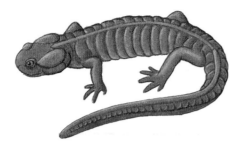

NORTHWEST SALAMANDER
(*Ambystoma gracile*)

Description. Adult a rich brown dorsally, with light gray belly and lighter-colored glandular areas behind eyes and along back and tail. Moist, smooth skin. Prominent grooves along sides. Total length including tail up to 9½ inches.
Distribution. Mostly found in low-elevation rivers and ponds, but reported in Rainier up to 5,725 feet at Sunrise Lake.
Remarks. Seldom seen, as it spends most of its time in underground burrows. In dry summer months, seeks shelter in rotten logs, caves, and other moist areas. Potent poison from skin glands that discourages predators.

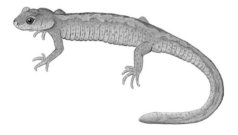

LONG-TOED SALAMANDER
(*Ambystoma macrodactylum*)

Description. Named for the very long fourth toe on its hind foot. Prominent grooves and ridges along sides. Smooth black or brown skin with greenish or yellow stripe extending along head, back, and tail. White speckling on sides.
Distribution. One of the most widely distributed salamanders, living in a variety of habitats from lowland forest to the subalpine. Found to 6,190 feet at Shadow Lake in the park.
Remarks. Introduced fish have decimated populations of this salamander elsewhere, since the fish consume the larvae.

WESTERN RED-BACKED SALAMANDER
(Plethodon vehiculum)

Description. Slender salamander about 4½ inches long including tail, with an even-edged dorsal stripe running from tip of tail to head. Sides are gray or black, belly is gray with white speckling.
Distribution. This salamander is the most widespread in the Pacific Northwest and is strongly associated with coniferous forests. It does not tolerate cold, hence is seldom found in areas where snow is common. Tends to be found near rocks, on talus slopes, beneath large logs.
Remarks. Eats primarily mites, spiders, and other invertebrates.

PACIFIC GIANT SALAMANDER
(Dicamptodon tenebrosus)

Description. Body to 7 inches. Bulky head and body. Marbled pattern on brown background, although some individuals lack marbling. Undersides tan.
Distribution. Cool, moist forests near streams or lakes.
Remarks. Jaws are strong enough to give a powerful bite. Typically active only after dark and when forests are moist.

VAN DYKE'S SALAMANDER
(Plethodon vandykei)

Description. This small salamander averages about 4 inches total length including tail. It has fourteen costal grooves (grooves and ridges on its sides). Toes are slightly webbed. The color is variable, even within the same population. It can be yellowish or reddish, or have dark sides with white speckling and a light stripe down the back.

Distribution. This salamander is only found in three regions of Washington, including Mount Rainier National Park. Though a woodland species and able to live far from water if in a moist environment, it is often found around seeps, waterfalls, and streams. It has been reported to 3,600 feet along the Carbon River in the park.

Remarks. Considered to be the most aquatic of woodland salamanders, but lays its eggs on land. Larval stage completed in egg, and young are born as miniature adults.

ENSATINA
(Ensatina eschscholtzii)

Description. Stout-bodied with twelve costal grooves. Tail has a distinct constriction at base. No dorsal stripe. Reddish, orangish, brown, or tan overall.

Distribution. Commonly found under woody debris and logs. Prefers drier habitat and avoids wet places. Has been reported to 3,800 feet in the Washington Cascades.

Remarks. When attacked, will wave its tail back and forth. Tail can break off and continue to wiggle, often distracting predator while ensatina makes its escape. The animal will grow a new tail.

WESTERN TOAD
(Bufo boreas)

Description. Large animal with horizontal eye pupils and dry, warty skin. Conspicuous oval parotid glands, enlarged areas at the back of the head where poison is excreted. Reddish to greenish, nearly always with a white stripe down the back. Underside pale with dark blotches.
Distribution. Common by lakes and ponds, but will travel through dry forest.
Remarks. Normally nocturnal, so seldom seen. Moves by crawling and climbing, rather than jumping. If attacked, will secrete a poison. Western Washington populations have experienced significant declines.

TAILED FROG
(Ascaphus truei)

Description. Small, 2-inch frog. Grayish green, reddish brown, or brown, with yellow and gray mottling. Male has prominent cloacal "tail." Eye has vertical pupil. No external ear.
Distribution. Found near cold, rocky streams. Not usually associated with ponds or lakes. Reported to 5,200 feet near Tipsoo Lake in the park.
Remarks. Seldom seen; nocturnal. Hides under rocks in daytime and comes out to hunt under cover of darkness. Has hardened toes to assist in crawling along rocky streams. The lack of an external ear is an adaptation to its typically noisy environment along rushing mountain streams, where hearing acuity is relatively unimportant. This frog has suffered population declines outside of the park due to sedimentation caused by logging.

RED-LEGGED FROG
(Rana aurora)

Description. Up to 4 inches. Reddish brown or brown, with small, black markings and spots on back and sides. Irregular black bands across legs. Usually has dark mask on head. Ventral side of legs red, sometimes extending up onto belly and sides. Creamy white throat.
Distribution. Woodlands adjacent to streams. Reported at 2,800 feet by Longmire Campground.
Remarks. It takes three to four years for frogs to reach sexual maturity.

PACIFIC TREE FROG
(Pseudacris regilla)

Description. Less than 2 inches. Brown, green, pale gray, or reddish. Conspicuous dark mask from nose to the shoulders. Often a Y-shaped pattern between eyes on top of head. Long, slender legs. Toes have round pads. (No other frog has toe pads.)
Distribution. The most common frog in Pacific Northwest. Found in a variety of habitats, from urban yards to deep forests. Often far from water.
Remarks. Males produce one prolonged note, particularly after rain, giving rise to common name "chorus frog."

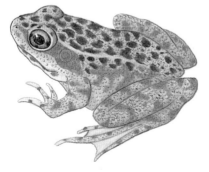

CASCADES FROG
(Rana cascadae)

Description. Total length up to 3 inches. Olive green, brown, or tan. Covered with black spots. Dark mask from eye to shoulder, with a lighter stripe along jaw from nose to shoulder. Ventral side of legs yellowish to gold.
Distribution. Associated with small pools and marshy areas adjacent to streams in subalpine terrain. Seldom found below 2,000 feet, and reported up to 6,120 feet at Shadow Lake in the park.
Remarks. Until 1939, considered to be the same species as the spotted frog.

Reptiles

Turtles, lizards, and snakes are all reptiles. All have adaptations for life on land, although some species, such as the western pond turtle and the garter snake, may be strongly associated with water. All reptiles have scales, and their young are born alive or in eggs. In either case, they don't require a water environment to reproduce as do amphibians.

Lizards and snakes differ from one another in several ways. Lizards (at least in the Pacific Northwest) have limbs with sharp claws, but snakes are limbless. Lizards have external ear openings and eyelids that can blink; snakes do not.

Because of the cool temperatures that dominate Mount Rainier, there are few reptiles found within the park. There are no poisonous species.

NORTHERN ALLIGATOR LIZARD
(*Elgaria coerulea*)

Description. A stout, dark brown or greenish brown lizard up to 10 inches total length. Longitudinal fold on each side of body. Square dorsal scales separated from a similar-shaped scale by a mid-body line of small scales. Eyes brown.
Distribution. Moist forests, forest openings, and clearings.
Remarks. Bears a litter of fully formed lizards.

RUBBER BOA
(*Charina bottae*)

Description. Usually less than 24 inches. Rubbery look and feel to skin. Vestiges of hind limbs called anal spurs. Back is uniform dark or light brown. Short, blunt tail that looks similar to the wedge-shaped head.
Distribution. Usually found near water, under logs, in rock crevices, and under leaf litter.
Remarks. Can climb and swim well. Usually nocturnal. Crushes its prey.

COMMON GARTER SNAKE
(Thamnophis sirtalis)

Description. May reach 52 inches in length. Great color variation, most commonly black dorsal color with black head and yellow-green vertebral stripe. Belly light green or blue near head, darkening to black near tail.
Distribution. Sea level to 6,000 feet. Wide variety of habitats, but usually associated with water, ponds, sloughs, and streams.
Remarks. If captured, will release feces, urine, and musk to discourage predator.

WESTERN GARTER SNAKE
(Thamnophis elegans)

Description. Up to 40 inches in length. Light gray to light brown dorsally, with dull yellow vertebral and lateral stripes, and light gray belly.
Distribution. Usually near water. Common near human habitation.
Remarks. One of the most aquatic garter snakes. Has the most varied diet of any snake, including leeches, snails, slugs, mice, voles, frogs, salamanders, and even small birds.

NORTHWESTERN GARTER SNAKE
(Thamnophis ordinoides)

Description. Small, usually less than 2 feet in length. Greatest color variation of any snake in Pacific Northwest, even among litter mates. Dorsal background color black, brown, gray, or olive. Vertebral stripe red, yellow, turquoise, white, or orange. Lateral stripes white or yellow. Relatively small head helps distinguish it from other garter snakes.
Distribution. Primarily terrestrial; found in thickets, meadows, forest clearings.
Remarks. Will forage in rain, seeking slugs, earthworms, frogs, salamanders, and snails.

BIRDS

Birds evolved from reptiles and still possess a few reptilian features, such as scaly feet. Their forelimbs evolved into wings, used by most birds for flying, but some seabirds, such as penguins, use the wings as flippers for swimming. A large breast bone provides a sturdy structure for the attachment of the huge flight muscles.

Birds are covered with feathers, which are modified scales. Feathers not only enable flight but also provide excellent insulation, an adaptation necessary for survival as a small-bodied, warm-blooded animal. Several other features also enable flight. Most birds have a honeycombed bone structure, which creates structural strength but not much weight. They have no teeth, which would add weight, but have lightweight bills designed for specific foods: hooked bills in predators; stout, heavy bills for crushing seeds in seedeaters; stout, pointed bills for drilling wood in woodpeckers; and long, thin bills in birds that probe sand or mudflats.

Because of the great caloric demands of flying, and the energy cost of maintaining their internal body temperature, most birds eat foods of a high calorie-to-weight value, including insects, seeds, nuts, and flesh. There are relatively few herbivores among bird species; most of these are larger ones, such as geese.

All birds are hatched from eggs and are given varying degrees of parental attention. Some species are precocial, able to run or swim almost immediately upon hatching. This includes some ducks, shorebirds, and chickenlike birds such as grouse. Most, however, are altricial, requiring a degree of parental care. Baby birds remain in the nest for days or weeks until they are fledged (have the feathers necessary for flying).

Most birds have variations in plumage that change with the season, sex, or state of development of the bird. For example, the male mallard duck

SPECIES LIST BY HABITAT

Lowland Forests

Cooper's hawk
sharp-shinned hawk
blue grouse
ruffed grouse
band-tailed pigeon
western screech owl
great horned owl
northern pygmy owl
spotted owl
northern saw-whet owl
Vaux's swift
red-breasted sapsucker
pileated woodpecker
hairy woodpecker
three-toed woodpecker
northern flicker
olive-sided flycatcher
Hammond's flycatcher
western wood-pewee

tree swallow
violet-green swallow
barn swallow
Steller's jay
gray jay
common raven
black-capped chickadee
chestnut-sided
  chickadee
brown creeper
dipper
winter wren
robin
Townsend's solitaire
varied thrush
Swainson's thrush
ruby-crowned kinglet
golden-crowned kinglet
solitary vireo

warbling vireo
orange-crowned warbler
Townsend's warbler
hermit warbler
common yellowthroat
Audubon's warbler
Wilson's warbler
western tanager
pine siskin
chipping sparrow
savannah sparrow
fox sparrow
song sparrow
Lincoln's sparrow
white-crowned sparrow
golden-crowned sparrow
red crossbill
dark-eyed junco

Subalpine Meadows and Forests

bald eagle
northern harrier
sharp-shinned hawk
Cooper's hawk
northern goshawk
red-tailed hawk
golden eagle
blue grouse
rufous hummingbird
hairy woodpecker
western wood-pewee
Pacific-slope flycatcher
horned lark
gray jay
Steller's jay

Clark's nutcracker
mountain chickadee
chestnut-backed
  chickadee
red-breasted nuthatch
winter wren
golden-crowned kinglet
ruby-crowned kinglet
hermit thrush
western bluebird
mountain bluebird
robin
varied thrush
American pipit
cedar waxwing

yellow-rumped warbler
Townsend's warbler
Wilson's warbler
chipping sparrow
fox sparrow
song sparrow
Lincoln's sparrow
white-crowned sparrow
golden-crowned sparrow
dark-eyed junco
gray-crowned rosy finch
red crossbill
pine siskin
evening grosbeak

Alpine Zone

white-tailed ptarmigan
gray-crowned rosy finch
common raven

has a green head, while the female is typically a mottled brown color. And some gulls have juvenile plumage that changes at different ages.

Flight provides birds with incredible mobility. More than any other animal group, birds are able to travel long distances relatively efficiently. Migration is one way birds cope with seasonal food shortages, inclement weather, and competition with other birds, and there are few year-round residents in northern zones. Most of the birds in Mount Rainier National Park are seasonal residents, breeding here in the summer but wintering elsewhere. Others breed farther north and are seen here only during spring or fall migrations.

Because birds are so mobile, they may be seen in many different habitats. However, most species still have a preferred habitat. The preceding table includes the birds that are most strongly associated with each habitat zone; many are frequently found in more than one zone.

Species Accounts

Several hundred species of birds are known to reside or migrate through the park. The following species accounts feature all the species known to breed in the park, plus a handful of nonbreeders that may be conspicuous during migration. For a comprehensive list of all known species, obtain the checklist of *Birds of Mount Rainier National Park,* available at National Park Service visitor centers. The species descriptions provided here are sketchy and may not be suitable for keying out each bird to the species level. To aid you in positive identification, consult a good birding guide.

Geese and Ducks

Geese and ducks are associated with water and typically have webbed feet. Geese have blunt, triangular bills. Sexes are alike. Ducks are divided into several subgroups including dabblers, or puddle ducks, and divers. Puddle ducks, such as mallards, are generally able to spring directly from the water into the air and can readily walk on land. Diving ducks have the legs set farther back on the body, which aids in underwater pursuit of prey but makes it more difficult to walk on land. When taking flight, they typically patter along the water's surface before becoming airborne. Seven species of ducks and geese have been reported for Mount Rainier National Park, but only three are resident breeders.

HARLEQUIN DUCK
(Histrionicus histrionicus)

Description. Smallish duck, up to 16 inches. Short bill. Male blue-gray with chestnut sides, white patch in front of eye, and other white bars and patches on head, neck, and wings. Female brownish with three round white spots on each side of head. Rapid flight.

Distribution. Nests on fast-moving streams and winters on coast. After eggs hatch, the male returns to the coast, leaving female to raise young alone.

Remarks. Rare breeding resident. Harlequin duck numbers are declining across their range outside of Alaska. Less than 1,500 ducks are thought to reside in the entire state of Washington. They are being considered for listing as an endangered species. In Rainier and other inland sites, harlequins feed on caddis fly larvae and other invertebrates they capture from the bottom of streams.

COMMON MERGANSER
(Mergus merganser)

Description. Medium duck, up to 27 inches. Male has greenish head, white body, and black back. When in flight, looks predominantly white. Female has crested rufous head, gray body, white throat and wing patch. Both have red serrated bill and red feet.

Distribution. Common on rivers, particularly larger ones. Occasionally seen on lakes.

Remarks. Rare. Breeds in park, nesting in cavities in trees near water. A fish-eating duck that captures prey by diving. To get airborne, patters on surface of the water for a long way prior to liftoff.

BARROW'S GOLDENEYE
(Bucephala islandica)

Description. Up to 18 inches. Male has a white body, black back, glossy purple head, and white crescent on face. Female has grayish body and brown head with white neck ring; all yellow bill during breeding season.

Distribution. Lakes and rivers.

Remarks. Rare. Breeds in park. A cavity nester. Feeds on small fish and invertebrates. After diving, bobs back to the surface like a cork. Named for Sir John Barrow, secretary to the British Admiralty, for whom Barrow, Alaska, also is named.

GOLDEN EAGLE
(Aquila chrysaetos)

Description. Large, brown bird, up to 40 inches, with a 7- to 8-foot wingspread. Immature birds have white in wings at base of primary feathers and at base of tail with dark terminal band; can be distinguished from immature bald eagles by the more conspicuous brightness of the white patches.

Distribution. Open subalpine and alpine terrain.

Remarks. Uncommon. Breeds in park. Soars along ridge lines and subalpine meadows looking for marmots and other rodents.

AMERICAN KESTREL
(Falco sparverius)

Description. Small falcon, 9 to 12 inches. Rusty back and tail with black bars. Black double mustache on face. Pointed wings, blue-gray in males.

Distribution. Open subalpine meadows.

Remarks. Occasional migrant. Frequently hovers. Feeds on insects and small rodents. Cavity nester. Previously known as "sparrow hawk."

Grouse and Quail

Grouse and quail are chickenlike birds with precocial young able to run within minutes of being born. Often seen on the ground.

BLUE GROUSE
(*Dendragapus obscurus*)

Description. Chickenlike, up to 20 inches. Male dusky gray to blackish with yellow or orange comb above eye. Female brownish. Square tail with light terminal band.
Distribution. Coniferous forests, particularly near timberline in winter.
Remarks. Common year-round, breeding resident. Breeding males produce loud, low *hoot, hoot, hoot* vocalizations, one of the earliest signs of spring.

RUFFED GROUSE
(*Bonasa umbellus*)

Description. Chickenlike, up to 19 inches. Red-brown; reddish tail with black band near tip.
Distribution. Coniferous forests, bushy woodlands, riparian areas, generally at lower elevations.
Remarks. Uncommon year-round, breeding resident. Breeding male drums wings on hollow logs, producing loud noise like a lawn mower starting up.

WHITE-TAILED PTARMIGAN
(*Lagopus leucurus*)

Description. Small, up to 13 inches. In summer, mottled brown with white wings, tail, and belly. In winter, all white, except for black eyes and beak.
Distribution. Alpine zone.
Remarks. Uncommon year-round breeding resident. Heavily feathered feet act as snowshoes. In extremely cold weather, will dive into soft snow, which insulates the bird from the most frigid temperatures.

Shorebirds

Shorebirds, as their name implies, are common along water. Most are chunky and active birds.

SPOTTED SANDPIPER
(Actitis macularia)

Description. Small, 7 to 8 inches. Olive-brown above, white breast with black spots during breeding season, white line over eye, white wing stripe and tip of tail. Teeters up and down constantly.
Distribution. Sandy and cobble beaches along lakes and streams.
Remarks. Uncommon. Breeds in park. Flies with stiff, rapid wingbeats. Unlike other sandpipers, which forage in large flocks, spotted sandpiper is usually solitary.

Pigeons

These are small-headed, plump, fast-flying birds. Only one species is found in the park.

BAND-TAILED PIGEON
(Columba fasciata)

Description. Resembles typical city pigeon, with broad, pale band across end of fanlike tail and white crescent on nape. Male is brown with pink-purple underparts and almost white abdomen.
Distribution. Forests, particularly Douglas fir. Prefers timber stands with some openings.
Remarks. Uncommon. Breeds in park. Strong, fast flier, often in flocks.

Owls

Owls are nocturnal birds of prey that hunt primarily by sound. They have short necks and large, forward-facing eyes. Six species have been reported for the park, all year-round residents of forested areas.

WESTERN SCREECH OWL
(Otus kennicottii)

Description. Small, 7 to 10 inches. Reddish brown with yellow eyes.
Distribution. Coniferous forests.
Remarks. Uncommon. Breeds in park, nesting in tree cavities. Hunts mice, insects, even bats. Named for naturalist Robert Kennicott, an early explorer of Alaska.

GREAT HORNED OWL
(Bubo virginianus)

Description. Large owl, up to 2 feet, with ear tufts. Dark brown, heavily barred below, white throat, yellow eyes.
Distribution. Coniferous forests.
Remarks. Uncommon. Breeds in park. Voice a deep *hoo-hoo-hoooo-hoo-hoo*. Sometimes seen in daylight. Glides, but seldom soars.

NORTHERN PYGMY OWL
(Glaucidium gnoma)

Description. Very small, brown owl, lacking ear tufts. Whitish belly with dark streaks. Small, white dots around head and face. Neck has black patch on either side, suggestive of eyes on back of head. Tail long and barred.
Distribution. Coniferous forests.
Remarks. Uncommon. Breeds in park, nesting in cavities. Very tame, easily approached. Often looks back with curious perky glance.

NORTHERN SPOTTED OWL
(Strix occidentalis)

Description. Medium size, up to 20 inches. Dark brown body with heavy white barring. Dark eyes.
Distribution. Old-growth forests.
Remarks. Uncommon. Breeds in park. The spotted owl is heading toward extinction due to the loss of old-growth forest habitat.

BARRED OWL
(Strix varia)

Description. Large, 17 to 24 inches. Rounded head without ear tufts. Gray-brown above and pale below, with dark barring across chest, vertical streaking on belly, and white spots on back. Dark eyes. Yellow bill.
Distribution. Coniferous forests.
Remarks. Uncommon. Breeds in park. Primarily an eastern species that has recently invaded the Pacific Northwest. Call sounds like "who cooks for you."

NORTHERN SAW-WHET OWL
(Aegolius acadicus)

Description. Small, 8-inch owl. Reddish brown with brown and white streaks below. Whitish between the eyes and over bill. No ear tufts.
Distribution. Coniferous forests.
Remarks. Uncommon. Breeds in park. Very tame. In taking off, drops slightly. If it kills more than it can eat, will store excess in trees for later consumption.

Swifts

These fast-flying, insect-feeding birds have long pointed wings bent close to the body. Two species are found in the park: the uncommon black swift and the more abundant Vaux's swift.

VAUX'S SWIFT
(Chaetura vauxi)

Description. Small, 4½-inch, grayish brown bird with pale white throat. Short, stubby tail and long, pointed wings.
Distribution. Coniferous forests up to timberline.
Remarks. Common. Breeds in park, nesting in tree cavities. Old-growth-dependent species. Cruises the treetops, devouring insects.

Hummingbirds

These tiny birds with needlelike bills hover at flowers to sip nectar. Only two species have been recorded for the park.

CALLIOPE HUMMINGBIRD
(Stellula calliope)

Description. Body 3 inches. Green back. Male has rose-purple stripes on throat. Female has white throat and belly.
Distribution. Meadows with forested edge up to timberline.
Remarks. Uncommon. Breeds in park. Smallest bird in North America, and smallest bird completing a major migration—flies up to 5,500 miles between summer breeding grounds and wintering areas. During courtship, males make repeated shallow Us in flight.

RUFOUS HUMMINGBIRD
(Selasphorus rufus)

Description. Body 3½ inches long. Male has reddish brown body with white across chest, green crown, and iridescent orange-red throat. Female has green back, white throat and belly, with brownish red on sides and by tail.
Distribution. Forest and subalpine meadows and basins.
Remarks. Common. Breeds in park. In July and August, many migrating hummingbirds from farther north concentrate on foraging for nectar in the flowering subalpine basins.

Kingfisher

This short-legged, chunky bird with a crest and a large, stout bill is found near ponds and streams. Only one species is found in most of the United States.

BELTED KINGFISHER
(Ceryle alcyon)

Description. About a foot long. Slate blue with ragged crest on large head; white neck ring, chest, and belly; grayish breast bands. Female also has rusty breast band.
Distribution. Near streams, ponds, and lakes.
Remarks. Uncommon. Breeds in park, nesting in burrows in streambanks. Hovers or rests in branch over stream or lake, then dives headfirst into water to capture fish. Voice a distinctive rattle.

Woodpeckers

Woodpeckers use their stout bills to chisel wood. They have stiff tail feathers, short legs, and strong claws. Eight woodpeckers have been reported for the park; all breed here.

LEWIS'S WOODPECKER
(Melanerpes lewis)

Description. Body 11 inches. Dark, greenish black head and back with gray-ish breast and collar, pinkish belly, and red face.
Distribution. Forests.
Remarks. Rare. Breeds in park. Named for Meriwether Lewis of the Lewis and Clark Expedition. Acts like a flycatcher, capturing insects on the wing.

RED-BREASTED SAPSUCKER
(Sphyrapicus ruber)

Description. Red head, breast, and neck. Black back, white wing patch and rump.
Distribution. Moist coniferous forests.
Remarks. Uncommon. Breeds in park. Feeds on ants attracted to sap from holes drilled in trees.

DOWNY WOODPECKER
(Picoides pubescens)

Description. Body 6 to 7 inches. Smallest woodpecker in North America. Head black with two white patches, one just behind eye, and red patch on back. White belly and back, black wings with white bars. Tail black; outer tail feathers white, with a few black bars. Has smaller bill than hairy woodpecker.
Distribution. Riparian forests, mixed conifer forests.
Remarks. Uncommon. Breeds in park.

HAIRY WOODPECKER
(Picoides villosus)

Description. Body 8 to 10 inches. Same coloration as downy woodpecker. Difficult to distinguish from downy other than larger size and longer, stouter bill.
Distribution. Coniferous forests.
Remarks. Common. Breeds in park. Diet mostly insects.

BLACK-BACKED WOODPECKER
(Picoides arcticus)

Description. Body 10 inches. Solid black back and barred sides. Male has yellow cap. White throat; mustache on side of face.
Distribution. Forests.
Remarks. Rare. Breeds in park. Flicks bark off dead trees to find insects, rather than drilling. Common among snags from recent fires.

NORTHERN FLICKER
(Colaptes auratus)

Description. Up to a foot long. Brown-and-blue-barred back and wings, lighter belly with black spots, black throat patch, gray head with red mustache.
Distribution. Subalpine and lowland coniferous forests.
Remarks. Common year-round, breeding resident. Feeds primarily on ants. Appears robinlike, often hopping and foraging on the ground.

PILEATED WOODPECKER
(Dryocopus pileatus)

Description. Crow-size black bird with pointed red crown, white stripes on face and down shoulder, white underwings visible in flight.
Distribution. Typically associated with old-growth coniferous forests.
Remarks. Uncommon year-round, breeding resident. Drills characteristic rectangular 2- to 4-inch holes in trees in pursuit of ants, its primary food source.

Flycatchers

Many of the species are difficult to distinguish from one another. All have bristles around the base of the bill. Flycatchers perch on branches and swoop down to capture flying insects. Six breeding species are found in the park; five are described here.

OLIVE-SIDED FLYCATCHER
(Contopus borealis)

Description. Body to 8 inches, with a short tail. Brownish olive above; throat, belly, and breast whitish yellow. Dark streaks on flanks and sometimes across breast. White tuft on rump.
Distribution. Coniferous forests up to subalpine zone.
Remarks. Uncommon year-round, breeding resident. Typically nests high in trees, often 50 feet or more. Forages from treetops, making dipping sweeps from branches in pursuit of insects.

WILLOW FLYCATCHER
(Empidonax traillii)

Description. Body to 6 inches. Green-brown above, with whitish throat, pale olive breast, and pale yellow belly.
Distribution. Near water in riparian areas.
Remarks. Rare. Breeds in park. Forages from branch to branch in dense shrubs. Call is distinctive *fitz-bew*. Often flicks tail upward.

WESTERN WOOD-PEWEE
(Contopus sordidulus)

Description. Body 6 inches, gray-brown above with olive-gray flanks and breast. Two narrow white wing bars.
Distribution. Low-elevation coniferous to subalpine forests.
Remarks. Occasional. Breeds in park. Tends to forage at mid elevations in forest canopy.

HAMMOND'S FLYCATCHER
(Empidonax hammondii)

Description. Body 5 to 6 inches. Has shorter tail than other flycatchers. Gray head, grayish olive sides, grayish white throat, white eye ring.
Distribution. Lowland coniferous and mixed deciduous-coniferous forests.
Remarks. Rare. Breeds in park. Nests in coniferous forests.

DUSKY FLYCATCHER
(Empidonax oberholseri)

Description. Body to 6 inches. Grayish olive above and on breast, throat whitish, underparts yellowish. Conspicuous white eye ring. Difficult to distinguish from Hammond's flycatcher.
Distribution. Forests up to subalpine.
Remarks. Rare. Breeds in park. Forages low to ground.

Larks

Larks have musical voices and are generally a dull brown color, with no differences between the sexes.

HORNED LARK
(Eremophila alpestris)

Description. Body size 7 to 8 inches. Overall brown color, but with black "horns" on head, black "whiskers" on face, black breast spots, pale yellow flanks, and pale belly.
Distribution. Open fields, particularly in subalpine and alpine terrain.
Remarks. Uncommon. Breeds in park. Walks or runs instead of hopping on ground. Its scientific name means "lark of the mountains."

Swallows

Swallows are sparrow size, streamlined birds with wide mouths and long, pointed wings. They spend most of their time in flight capturing insects on the wing. Three species of swallows have been reported for the park.

VIOLET-GREEN SWALLOW
(Tachycineta thalassina)

Description. Body 5 to 6 inches. Violet-green above, clear white below, extending up over eyes. White patches on rump.
Distribution. Usually near water, associated with subalpine openings.
Remarks. Common. Breeds in park. Highest forager of the swallows; often flies 100 feet high or more.

TREE SWALLOW
(Tachycineta bicolor)

Description. Body size 5 to 6 inches. Iridescent green-blue above with white below.
Distribution. Near water, in open areas and fields, and around deciduous forests.
Remarks. Occasional. Breeds in park, nesting in cavities. Does well where there is an abundance of snags.

BARN SWALLOW
(Hirundo rustica)

Description. Blue-black above, buffy underneath with rusty-red throat and face. Deeply forked tail.

Distribution. Near water. Often found in the forested lower elevations.

Remarks. Common. Breeds in park. Often associated with houses, bridges, barns, and other structures, where it constructs mud nests under eaves and overhangs.

Jays, Crows, and Ravens

These medium to large, intelligent birds have pointed bills, rounded wings, and generally loud calls. Five species have been reported for the park, but only three are common.

GRAY JAY
(Perisoreus canadensis)

Description. Body about a foot long. Gray overall, but darker on back. Dark cap. Throat, forehead, and collar white. Pale underparts.

Distribution. Low-elevation coniferous to subalpine forests.

Remarks. Abundant year-round breeding resident. Lays eggs in midwinter, often as early as February. Very tame. Called "camp robber" for its habit of invading picnic areas and campsites to pick up scraps.

Wrens

Wrens are small, chunky birds with slender bills. Their tails are often tipped at a jaunty angle. Only one species has been reported for the park.

WINTER WREN
(Troglodytes troglodytes)

Description. Body almost 5 inches. Stubby tail, brown body with barring on belly.

Distribution. Dense forests, among downfall, and in dense riparian vegetation.

Remarks. Common year-round, breeding resident. Active little bird that aggressively defends territory. Song is melodious trill that lasts eight seconds or more.

Dippers

These stocky birds are common along mountain streams. There is only one species in North America.

AMERICAN DIPPER
(Cinclus mexicanus)

Description. Body up to 8 inches. Gray-blue body with short tail and wings.

Distribution. Along fast mountain streams.

Remarks. Uncommon year-round, breeding resident. Has musical, wrenlike trill. Walks underwater feeding on aquatic insects.

Kinglets

Kinglets are tiny, active birds with small, slender bills and short tails.

GOLDEN-CROWNED KINGLET
(Regulus satrapa)

Description. Body 4 inches. Plump little bird with grayish olive upper body and white underparts, two white wing bars, and white eye stripe. Male has orange-yellow crown patch and female has yellow.
Distribution. Coniferous forests.
Remarks. Common year-round, breeding resident. Smallest songbird in North America.

RUBY-CROWNED KINGLET
(Regulus calendula)

Description. Body to 5 inches. Plump grayish olive bird with two white wing bars and white eye rings. Male has red crown patch, but it is seldom visible.
Distribution. Coniferous forests.
Remarks. Common. Breeds in park.

Thrushes

Thrushes are the familiar melodious songbirds of woodlands.

SWAINSON'S THRUSH
(Catharus ustulatus)

Description. Body to 7 inches. Brown above with streaked or spotted breast, white underparts, and light-colored eye ring.
Distribution. Moist woodlands and riparian vegetation.
Remarks. Common. Breeds in park. Song is a slow, rising spiral upward.

MACGILLIVRAY'S WARBLER
(Oporornis tolmiei)

Description. Grayish olive back, wings, and tail. Male has bluish gray head and bib, with black on lower part of throat and upper breast. Belly yellow. Female head is lighter gray, with no black on breast or throat.
Distribution. Dense shrubs and thickets.
Remarks. Uncommon. Breeds in park. Nests on ground.

COMMON YELLOWTHROAT
(Geothlypis trichas)

Description. Body up to 6 inches. Olive-brown crown, back, wings, and tail; yellow throat and flank; white belly. Male has black mask on face.
Distribution. Streamside thickets.
Remarks. Occasional. Breeds in park. Song distinctive *witch-ity, witch-ity.*

WILSON'S WARBLER
(Wilsonia pusilla)

Description. Body 5 inches. Bright yellow underparts, olive-brown back. Male has black cap.
Distribution. Woodland thickets along streams up to subalpine timberline.
Remarks. Common. Breeds in park. Nests on the ground amid brush.

Tanagers

Birds of tropical origins. Males are often brightly colored. Feed on insects and berries.

WESTERN TANAGER
(Piranga ludoviciana)

Description. Body 6 to 7 inches. Male is yellow with red head and black back, wings, and tail. White wing bars and yellow shoulder bars. Female yellowish below, olive above; lacks red head.
Distribution. Coniferous forests.
Remarks. Uncommon. Breeds in park. Tame around people.

Sparrows

This is a large group of small to medium-size birds with conical bills. Most species are difficult to distinguish by casual observation.

CHIPPING SPARROW
(Spizella passerina)

Description. Body to 6 inches. Mottled brown back, light gray underparts, prominent reddish brown cap, black line through eye, and white eyebrow.
Distribution. Forests and edges of sub-alpine meadows.
Remarks. Uncommon. Breeds in park. Named for its high-pitched *chip*.

SAVANNAH SPARROW
(Passerculus sandwichensis)

Description. Olive-brown back streaked with black, black-spotted chest, white underparts, pink legs and feet.
Distribution. Open country such as subalpine meadows.
Remarks. Uncommon. Breeds in park. Hops, rarely walks.

BROWN-HEADED COWBIRD
(*Molothrus ater*)

Description. Body 8 inches. Male glossy black with light brown head. Female gray-brown with light streaking on underparts.
Distribution. Forests and subalpine.
Remarks. Rare. Breeds in park. Nest parasite, laying eggs in nests of other songbirds, which then raise young as if they were their own. Widespread farming and forest fragmentation by logging have expanded the range of this bird.

Finches

Finches are seedeaters with undulating flight.

CASSIN'S FINCH
(*Carpodacus cassinii*)

Description. Body 6 inches. Reddish crown, throat, and rump. Brown nape and whitish belly.
Distribution. Low-elevation and subalpine spruce-fir forests.
Remarks. Occasional. Breeds in park. Named for John Cassin, a nineteenth-century bird taxonomist.

GRAY-CROWNED ROSY FINCH
(*Leucosticte tephrocotis*)

Description. Body to 6 inches. Sexes similar. Brown chest and back, rosy belly, black forehead, and gray crown.
Distribution. Subalpine and alpine meadows.
Remarks. Common. Breeds in park. Nests on tundra.

PINE SISKIN
(Carduelis pinus)

Description. Body to 5 inches. Brown-streaked body with yellow wing marks visible in flight. Yellow at base of tail.
Distribution. Coniferous forests.
Remarks. Common year-round, breeding resident. Often forms large flocks in winter.

PURPLE FINCH
(Carpodacus purpureus)

Description. Body is not purple, despite name. Reddish over most of male body, back streaked with brown, pale white belly, wings brownish. Female heavily streaked brown bird with pale, streaked underparts. Notched tail. Stout bill.
Distribution. Coniferous forests, open woodlands.
Remarks. Occasional. Breeds in park.

RED CROSSBILL
(Loxia curvirostra)

Description. Male dull red with brown wings. Female yellowish brown. Distinctive feature is crossed bill. Notched short tail.
Distribution. Coniferous forests.
Remarks. Uncommon year-round, breeding resident. Uses its crossed bill to extract pine seeds from cones. Nomadic birds that search in flocks for abundant cone crops.

Grosbeaks

Grosbeaks are larger, finchlike seedeaters with thick, strong bills.

BLACK-HEADED GROSBEAK
(Pheucticus melanocephalus)

Description. Body to 7¾ inches. Male has orange-brown breast, collar, and rump; black head and wings, with white wing bars. Female dark brown above and light tan-ochre below, with crown stripes.
Distribution. Forests.
Remarks. Rare. Breeds in park. Outstanding singer.

EVENING GROSBEAK
(Coccothraustes vespertinus)

Description. Body 8 inches. Male golden yellow, dark head with black crown and yellow eyebrow. Female has gray head and back and yellowish underparts. Both sexes have stout, light-colored bill, black wings and tail, white wing patches.
Distribution. Forests and subalpine areas.
Remarks. Occasional. Breeds in park. *Vespertinus* in Latin means "of the evening," referring to its tendency to sing in the twilight hours.

MAMMALS

At least fifty species of mammals are known to reside in or near Mount Rainier National Park. Nevertheless, since most mammals are active at dusk or at night, few of the park's mammal species are observed by visitors.

Mammals are warm-blooded animals that bear live young (with the exception of the egg-laying duckbill platypus) and have fur that provides insulation. Insulation and warm-bloodedness enable mammals to exploit many habitats unsuitable for cold-blooded animals, such as the higher slopes of Mount Rainier. And mammals are able to remain active in the cooler nighttime hours, allowing the cover of night to provide protection from predators.

Mammals can be herbivores, or plant eaters, such as rabbits, rodents, and larger ungulates like deer, elk, and mountain goats; carnivores, or meat eaters, such as mountain lions, coyotes, and martens; or omnivores, plant and meat eaters, such as humans and bears. Most herbivores have teeth modified for grinding or chewing plant material, as well as long, modified intestinal tracts that allow more time for the digestion of coarse vegetable matter. For example, deer and elk have a four-parted stomach known as rumen, inoculated with special bacteria that aid digestion of fibrous plant material. Carnivores generally have teeth designed for cutting, tearing, and crushing flesh and bone, and shorter, more simplified digestive systems.

For most mammals, summer at Rainier is but a short reprieve from the dominant season of winter cold and snow. Cold and snow both require more energy of animals, and for herbivores, plant food becomes scarcer, if not completely unavailable. Mammals living in the park have adaptations that permit them to survive the winter season. Some, like deer and elk, avoid the worst winter conditions by migrating to lower elevations.

Shrews

Shrews are small, mouselike animals, typically with very pointed snouts and small eyes and ears. They also can be distinguished from mice by the canine nature of their upper incisor teeth—a feature you're only likely to observe on a dead specimen. They are largely insectivorous, feeding on insects and other invertebrates. They are, however, fierce predators that prey upon salamanders and earthworms. In many species, the life of adults is very short—most species live no more than a year and a half. After breeding and the young are weaned, most of the adults die, and almost the entire population consists of juveniles. Shrews live hidden beneath the forest litter, spending most of their life searching for food. Because of their very high metabolic rate, shrews must eat every two or three hours to maintain their body temperature. As a consequence, they must consume their own weight in prey every day or they will starve.

MASKED SHREW
(Sorex cinereus)

Description. Pointed snout. Fur velvety with light tan belly and sides, light brown back, and bicolor tail. Total length 5 inches with tail.
Distribution. Humid forested habitat, particularly at mid elevations. Not abundant in the park.
Remarks. One of the smallest of shrews. Eats insects, snails, earthworms, and other invertebrates.

TROWBRIDGE SHREW
(*Sorex trowbridgii*)

Description. Overall length 5 inches or so, half of which is tail. Pointed snout. Darker than other shrews. Sooty gray color, only slightly lighter on belly. Distinctive white-tan feet. Sharply bicolored tail brown above, white below.

Distribution. Forest dwellers. Abundant, particularly on western slopes, generally at low to mid elevations. Found in a wide variety of habitats, including forest floor litter, under logs and other cover, often far from water. More common in drier forests, a habitat less used by other shrews.

Remarks. Eats insects and other invertebrates, but also consumes conifer seeds. *Trowbridgii* is a proper name and refers to W. P. Trowbridge, who collected the first specimen near Astoria, Oregon, in 1855.

WANDERING SHREW
(*Sorex vagrans*)

Description. Small size, 4½ inches total, with tail about 1½ inches long. Strikingly different summer and winter fur color. In summer, light brown with pale grayish wash to undersides; in winter, sooty, almost black.

Distribution. Widely distributed, under logs and in dense vegetation in forests, meadows, and along lakeshores. Prefers moist habitats. Reaches greatest abundance in park at about 4,000 feet, but found up to 6,000 feet.

Remarks. Species name *vagrans* refers to wandering habit. Eats earthworms, insects, and other invertebrates. Along with the dusky shrew, one of the most numerous shrew species in the park.

SHREW MOLE
(*Neurotrichus gibbsii*)

Description. Smallest mole in North America. Total length about 5 inches, including a 1½-inch tail. Often mistaken for a shrew. Unlike other moles, feet longer than broad. Fur iridescent gray to black. Thick tail, scaly with bristlelike hairs; other moles have naked tails.
Distribution. Most abundant of mole species in Rainier, but still not common. Found in lower-elevation humid forests and along stream bottoms to 5,000 feet.
Remarks. Unlike other moles, does not create a burrow system but makes shallow, loose tunnels under logs and near the surface of loose soil thatched with decaying vegetation. May forage above ground in daylight. Able to swim quite well.

TOWNSEND'S MOLE
(*Scapanus townsendii*)

Description. Compact body, up to 8 inches long. Short, round, nearly naked tail 1 to 2 inches long. Flat, broad, pale front feet. Minute eyes and long, tapering naked pink snout. Metallic luster to velvety smooth, dark brown-black fur.
Distribution. Rather rare in the park. Tends to be found at lower elevations in damp, easily worked soils in fields and meadows such as the lawns at Longmire. Also reported along Ohanapecosh and Carbon River drainages.
Remarks. Largest North American mole. In 1897, the Biological Survey reported the unusual capture of a Townsend's mole at 5,000 feet in Spray Park.

COAST MOLE
(Scapanus orarius)

Description. Smaller than Townsend's mole, less than 5½ inches. Fur brownish black. Tail and snout nearly naked. Front paw as broad as that of Townsend's mole, but claws more slender. Reddish hind feet.

Distribution. Primarily a forest dweller, hence more common in Rainier than other moles, though still relatively rare. Also seen in meadows above 4,000 feet, such as at Spray Park and the Owyhigh Lakes.

Remarks. Preys heavily on earthworms.

Bats

Bats, which resemble mice with wings, are the only mammals that can truly fly. (Other animals, such as flying squirrels, glide.) Bats' wings are thin membranes of skin stretched between four greatly elongated "fingers" on each arm and the hind legs. The sternum is keeled like those of birds to accommodate the large flight muscles. All bats in the park are insectivorous, but in other parts of the world, bats also eat fruit, nectar, and even fish. Bats are nocturnal and take advantage of a vacant niche, the air space occupied by insect-feeding birds in the daytime. Because of their small body size, bats have a high metabolic rate. When not active, the bat lowers its body temperature and goes into a state of torpor. Most bats mate in the late autumn, but the females store the sperm for several months, and fertilization of eggs occurs in the spring.

Although bats have good eyesight—the old cliché "blind as a bat" is inaccurate—they do rely upon an extraordinary sense of hearing and echolocation (locating objects by means of reflected sound waves) to catch prey and avoid obstacles in the dark. So acute is their echolocation ability that in laboratory studies, bats have demonstrated an ability to distinguish between real and fake insects. Depending on hunting styles and prey, bats differ in ear size and the kinds of sonar signals emitted. Fast-flying bats, such as hoary bats, emit loud, high-frequency signals and have small ears. The western big-eared bat, which locates nonmoving insects on leaves, has very large ears and emits faint, soft signals.

Although most people associate bats with caves, many species crawl under the rough bark of large trees or roost inside hollow snags. Old-growth forests are important not only for spotted owls, but also for bats.

BIG BROWN BAT
(Eptesicus fuscus)

Description. One of the larger bat species in Rainier. Wingspan to 12 inches. Fur long, dark chocolate brown, and glossy. Blackish feet, ears, nose, and wing membrane. Short ears.

Distribution. In Rainier found primarily at lower elevations, seldom above 5,000 feet.

Remarks. Appears long before dark, feeding on beetles and other insects. Hibernates in the park but occasionally breaks torpor to forage, even in winter.

HOARY BAT
(Lasiurus cinereus)

Description. Wingspan to 14 inches. Short, round ears edged in black. Tail membrane heavily furred dorsally. Underparts yellowish to brown with frosted silver hairs. White patches of fur at "elbow" and "wrist."

Distribution. Moderate populations in the park. Forested habitats at low to mid elevations.

Remarks. Feeds high above the canopy, hundreds of feet above the ground. Migratory; summers in north, winters in south.

Rabbits, Hares, and Pikas

Rabbits are naked, blind, and helpless at birth, but hares are born fully furred, with eyes open and able to run. Hares do not dig burrows like rabbits, but hide in vegetation. Only one member of the hare family is native to Rainier, the snowshoe hare, although cottontail rabbits have been introduced into areas surrounding the park. Snowshoe hares exhibit periodic population cycles of nine to ten years, with numbers reaching high levels, then crashing. The pika looks like a smaller version of a rabbit, with tiny ears. It is often seen scurrying among boulders and rocks.

SNOWSHOE HARE
(Lepus americanus)

Description. Medium-size hare with short ears and large feet. Those found below 3,000 feet remain brown year-round, but those at higher elevations change to white in winter.
Distribution. Throughout the park, from lowlands to subalpine up to about 6,000 feet.
Remarks. Has a variety of vocalizations and communications, including a chirp, birdlike warble, distress cry, and thump on ground with foot.

PIKA
(Ochotona princeps)

Description. Small, 6- to 8-inch rabbit-like body with round, short ears. Tail not visible. Grayish brown with lighter underparts.
Distribution. Rockslides and talus slopes near subalpine and alpine meadows up to 8,000 feet.
Remarks. Quite active in daytime and often observed. Has sharp warning *ekk!* Gathers grass and flowers all summer and dries them in tiny "haystacks" sheltered under rocks for winter consumption.

Marmots

Marmots are members of the groundhog family. They are burrowing animals that live among rockpiles found in the alpine and subalpine zones. Only one species is found in the park.

HOARY MARMOT
(Marmota caligata cascadensis)

Description. Rotund, groundhoglike animal with head and body up to 20 inches, 7- to 10-inch tail, and short legs. Mixed white, gray, and black shoulders and head, with white belly and black feet. Waddles when running.
Distribution. Rocky talus slopes and meadows between 4,000 and 8,000 feet.
Remarks. Lives in colonies with a dominant male and several females and offspring. If alarmed, gives a shrill whistle. True hibernators that must put on a thick layer of fat to fuel the body during the cold months.

Hoary marmot. These members of the groundhog family live in colonies and emit a loud whistle when danger is sighted.

The golden-mantled ground squirrel looks like a chipmunk, but lacks the facial stripes of those smaller rodents.

Ground Squirrels

Ground squirrels are small to medium-size rodents that burrow underground. Only one species is found in the park.

GOLDEN-MANTLED
GROUND SQUIRREL
(*Spermophilus lateralis*)

Description. Chipmunklike but larger, and lacks stripes on face. Head and body 7 to 8 inches, with 3- to 4-inch tail. Buffy colored body, reddish brown head, white stripes on back, bordered by black.
Distribution. Prefers drier eastern side of mountain, from 3,000 feet up to timberline. Common at Sunrise Village area.
Remarks. Hibernates in winter.

Chipmunks

Chipmunks are small, active rodents with striped bodies and heads, and internal cheek pouches in which to carry food. They live in underground burrows and spend most of their time on the ground but are good climbers.

TOWNSEND'S CHIPMUNK
(*Tamias townsendii*)

Description. The larger of the two chipmunk species in the park. Body and head 6 inches, with a 4-inch tail. Dark, blackish stripes on a tawny background. Frosted white tail. Evident white eye stripe. Back of ears bicolored.
Distribution. Tends to reside in low-elevation forests.
Remarks. Stores seeds in its cheek pouch, then eats them in the safety of its burrow or on a log from which it can scan for predators.

YELLOW-PINE CHIPMUNK
(*Eutamias amoenus*)

Description. Smaller and lighter in color than Townsend's chipmunk. Head and body to 4½ inches with a 3½-inch tail. Ears unicolored on back. Black stripes continue to base of tail. Tail lacks white frosting of Townsend's.
Distribution. Prefers meadows at mid to high elevations.
Remarks. Quite nervous. Some biologists consider the yellow-pine chipmunk a subspecies of the least chipmunk.

Tree Squirrels

Tree squirrels are primarily arboreal and are exceptional climbers that are often seen leaping from branch to branch. They remain active all winter.

DOUGLAS SQUIRREL or CHICKAREE
(*Tamiasciurus douglasii*)

Description. Head and body to 7 inches, with a 6-inch tail. Back and sides grayish brown, with median band of rusty brown and black line on sides. Belly buffy-gray to rusty brown. Bushy tail brownish edged with black and light-colored tip.

Distribution. Very common in all coniferous forests.

Remarks. Also known as chickaree. Only tree squirrel you're likely to see in the daytime. A real chatterbox that often makes loud scolding sounds if humans or predators enter its territory. Stores cones in caches under tree roots. Hibernates in winter but occasionally rouses on warm, sunny days and scampers about digging out cached food.

NORTHERN FLYING SQUIRREL
(*Glaucomys sabrinus*)

Description. Head and body to 6 inches, with 4- to 5-inch tail. Skin folds between front and hind legs for gliding. Soft, cinnamon-gray fur on back and sides, underparts lighter to pale white. Large eyes.

Distribution. Found in all park forests, particularly older, mature forests.

Remarks. A nocturnal species, not likely to be seen in daylight. Doesn't truly fly, but glides from tree to tree with outstretched legs pulling folds of skin taut, acting as wings. A snag dweller that requires large, old trees for its nest. A favored prey of northern spotted owls.

Wood Rats

Wood rats have large ears and eyes, typically white feet, and hairy tails. When frightened, they thump with their hind feet. At least seven species of wood rats are found in North America, only one of which is found in the park.

BUSHY-TAILED WOOD RAT
(Neotoma cinerea)

Description. Head and body to 9 inches, with a 5- to 7-inch tail. Tail bushy like a squirrel's. Pale gray upper parts, whitish underparts, white hind feet, bicolored tail with gray above and white below.
Distribution. Uncommon; found throughout mid elevations, particularly around huts.
Remarks. Makes large nests of twigs, leaves, and other materials in rock crevices. Also known as a pack rat for its habit of carrying off objects, particularly bright colored paper, pieces of metal, and other "treasures."

Voles

Voles are small, mouselike animals with tails shorter than the body. Six species are found in the park.

GAPPER RED-BACKED VOLE
(Clethrionomys gapperi)

Description. Mouselike with shorter tail. Head and body $3\frac{1}{2}$ to $4\frac{1}{2}$ inches, with 2-inch tail. Brownish red band of hair on back.
Distribution. Common. Found in forests between 3,000 and 6,000 feet.
Remarks. Nests on the ground under stumps and logs.

HEATHER VOLE
(Phenacomys intermedius)

Description. Head and body to 4½ inches with a 1- to 1½-inch tail. Tail usually less than half body length. Gray-brown on back and sides, with silver-white belly and lower flank. Yellowish nose. Tail sharply bicolored, light below, dark above.

Distribution. Typically found in open meadows between 3,000 and 8,000 feet.

Remarks. Common meadow "mouse" found in flowery meadows of park.

OREGON MEADOW VOLE
(Microtus oregoni)

Description. Head and body about 4½ inches, with 1-inch tail. Sooty gray to brown upper body with paler gray belly. Tiny black ears, smaller than heather vole, barely protruding above fur.

Distribution. Found in both meadows and wooded areas.

Remarks. Schamberger says there are two varieties in Rainier, a smaller low-elevation animal and one found at higher elevations.

LONG-TAILED VOLE
(Microtus longicaudus)

Description. Head and body to 4 inches. Tail up to 3 inches. Long tail diagnostic. Reddish brown with blackish cast on back and on top of bicolored tail.

Distribution. Uncommon; found along western side of park at lower elevations, seldom above 3,500 feet.

Remarks. A tree-dwelling species that inhabits low-elevation meadows, which are not common in Rainier.

Raccoons

These medium-size carnivores are the only mammal with long, ringed tails and black masks. They walk on the entire foot, not just the toes.

RACCOON
(Procyon lotor)

Description. Head and body to 33 inches. Tail up to 12 inches. Generally grayish brown, with black face mask and black rings on bushy tail.
Distribution. Not abundant but present along streams below 4,000 feet.
Remarks. Lacking salivary glands, raccoons wash their food to help it slide down their throats.

Weasels, Skunks, and Allies

Members of the weasel family all have anal scent glands, best developed in the skunks. All have longish bodies, short legs, and small, rounded ears. Seven members of the weasel family have been reported in the park.

MARTEN
(Martes americana)

Description. Head and body up to 17 inches, with an 8- to 9-inch tail. Fur is a rich dark brown overall, with an orange or buff throat patch.
Distribution. Found throughout the park, but most common from 3,000 to 6,000 feet. Occasionally ventures into meadows far from forest cover.
Remarks. Often curious. Feeds on squirrels, voles, and occasionally berries.

FISHER
(Martes pennanti)

Description. Head and body 20 to 25 inches; bushy tail up to 15 inches. Blackish brown with black legs and tail.
Distribution. Mixed conifer-deciduous forests. Rare; may have been locally extirpated.
Remarks. Fishers have declined across much of their western U.S. range. Between 1955 and 1993 there were only 89 reports of fishers in the entire state of Washington, and only three were supported by photos or carcasses. The biggest factor is habitat loss due to clear-cutting, although some are also taken by trapping. Solitary animals outside of the breeding season, their numbers were never very large.

SHORT-TAILED WEASEL (ERMINE)
(Mustela erminea)

Description. Head and body to 9 inches in males (females slightly smaller), with a 3- to 4-inch tail. Very thin, lithe body with short legs. Brown with a creamy belly in summer, white in winter. Black-tipped tail.
Distribution. Common below 6,000 feet in all habitats where rodents are found.
Remarks. Very quick, often curious. Will scamper on snow surface, then dive down into hole to search for small voles and other prey.

LONG-TAILED WEASEL
(Mustela frenata)

Description. Larger than short-tailed weasel. Head and body to 10½ inches in males (females smaller), with an 4- to 6-inch tail. Short legs and longish body. Brown above with yellowish white below. Black-tipped tail. Some have white patches behind eyes. Turns white in winter at higher elevations.
Distribution. Rather uncommon. Generally found in open forests and meadows up to 6,000 feet.
Remarks. Preys upon voles and mice, but also kills bigger prey like pocket gophers and mountain beavers in their burrows.

MINK
(Mustela vison)

Description. Head and body to 17 inches, with a 7- to 9-inch furry tail. Short legs and longish body. Dark brown fur with white patch on chin. Does not turn white in winter.
Distribution. Uncommon; scattered individuals along lower-elevation streams, although can be found a considerable distance from water.
Remarks. Feeds on fish, frogs, salamanders, and even small birds. When cornered, the mink will sometimes emit a strong odor.

SPOTTED SKUNK
(Spilogale putorius)

Description. Head and body about 9 to 13 inches with 5- to 9-inch bushy tail. Black with four to six white stripes broken into spots or blotches. White spot on forehead and one under each ear. Tip of tail white.
Distribution. Brushy habitat. Found at low elevations on western side of park.
Remarks. The only skunk species common in the park. If cornered, turns and lifts hindquarters and sprays assailant with strong scent.

STRIPED SKUNK
(Mephitis mephitis)

Description. Head and body to 18 inches, with bushy 10-inch tail. About the size of a housecat. Black with white V down back.
Distribution. Western U.S. near streams. Status in Rainier uncertain. Found in low-elevation areas of western Washington, and potentially could be found on the fringes of the park at the lowest elevations.
Remarks. Can spray its scent up to 25 feet. Feeds on grubs, beetles, small mammals, worms, and bird eggs.

Bull elk in velvet. There is some dispute about whether elk were native to Mount Rainier. Elk are most common on the eastern side of the park.

BLACK-TAILED DEER
(*Odocoileus hemionus*)

Description. Reddish color in summer, grayish brown in winter. Black-tipped tail. Males have branched antlers. Weight up to 250 pounds, but many, particularly females, are quite a bit smaller.
Distribution. Throughout the park, from forests to meadows. Subalpine meadows at Sunrise and Paradise are usually good places to see deer in summer.
Remarks. Typically eat browse, rather than grass, although wildflowers are a big part of the summer diet. Most of the deer in the park are migratory, moving upslope in summer to feed upon lush vegetation, and descending to winter in forested lowlands.

Mountain Goats

Mountain goats are actually related to antelope. They live on steep slopes and are remarkably agile climbers. Their chief defense against predators is their ability to scale sheer cliffs. Both sexes have horns (as opposed to antlers, which are shed each year). Females with kids occupy the best habitat and staunchly defend it against all other goats, including males. Their sharp horns are lethal weapons, and female goats are able to discourage most other goats from advancing onto their territory. Avalanches and falling are the chief causes of mortality.

MOUNTAIN GOAT
(Oreamnos americanus)

Description. Stocky, white animal with foot-long, pointed black horns in both sexes.
Distribution. Found in high, rocky, alpine areas.
Remarks. Mountain goats are native to the Cascades.

Wildlife and Food

There are black bears in the park, and keeping them away from your food should be a major concern, not so much for your sake, but for theirs, as a bear habituated to human food often winds up having conflicts with humans and may be killed. For the sake of the bears, you should make every effort to keep your food inaccessible to them.

It's a wise idea to carry an extra stuff sac or other bag, along with some light cord for hanging food. Some of the designated wilderness campsites are equipped with poles for hanging food. If no poles exist, string your food up in a tree. If above timberline, try to put it on a steep cliff face.

Summit Climbing

Climbing Mount Rainier is something of a pilgrimage for many people. As one of the highest peaks in the lower forty-eight, and the one with the most commanding presence of any summit outside of Alaska, people are naturally drawn to the mountain. To climb the mountain, you must first obtain a permit.

Climbing Rainier is not to be taken lightly. There are crevasses, and glacier travel is required on all routes. Crampons, an ice ax, and ropes are necessities. It is not safe to climb solo; a summit attempt is best done in groups of three or more.

The weather on top of the 14,000-foot mountain can be severe. Many climbers are fooled by the benign Pacific Northwest climate and do not take along adequate clothing for the harsh conditions that may be encountered on top. When I climbed the mountain, I was surprised by how cold it was on the summit. I was not able to linger long before I had to retreat to warmer, lower elevations.

All water sources are frozen at higher elevations, and the thin air dehydrates the climber quickly. Take at least three quarts of water with you on the summit climb.

The two most popular routes are the Muir Camp–Ingraham Glacier and the Camp Schurman–Emmons Glacier climbs, both two-day trips. The Muir-Ingraham route begins at Paradise Meadows. Climbers ascend to Camp Muir at approximately 10,000 feet and camp for the night. There is a small hut where you can get out of the wind, but most parties set up camps. There is also a solar-powered outhouse here. Those heading to the summit usually begin their climb between 1 and 3 A.M. to take advantage of firm snow. The first part of the route crosses the Cowlitz Glacier and

View of Mount Adams from slope of Mount Rainier.

then goes up the Ingraham Glacier. The route changes from week to week, as new crevasses open and old ones close. It is a full day's climb round-trip from Camp Muir to the summit. Allow six to eight hours for the ascent and two to three for descent.

The Schurman-Emmons route is considered easier, but is longer. Most people allot 2½ days for the climb. The first day, hikers reach Glacier Basin and camp. From there, they move up to Schurman Hut Camp. The final push for the summit requires an early start, usually between 1 and 4 A.M., and follows the Corridor, a smooth ridge between the Winthrop and Emmons Glaciers that leads to the summit.

Hiking in the Park

All hike descriptions provided here are brief and are designed to give you a basic idea of what to expect on each trail. For more detailed trail descriptions, purchase one of the excellent hiking guides to Mount Rainier or stop in a visitor center to obtain more information.

Paradise Area

Nisqually Vista Trail: This 1.2-mile round-trip hike, starting by the Henry M. Jackson Visitor Center, climbs up through the flower-studded Paradise Meadows and offers excellent views of Mount Rainier and the Nisqually Glacier.

Bench and Snow Lakes Trail: After an initial climb, this 2.5-mile round-trip trail levels out, providing access to two lakes. Bench Lake is reached in 0.8 mile, and Snow Lake is another 0.5 mile farther. The trail climbs through flowery meadows that are thick with showy beargrass in July. Good views of Mount Rainier are seen from the trail. The trailhead is located 1 mile east of Reflection Lake on the Stevens Canyon Road.

Alta Vista Trail: This 1.5-mile round-trip loop starts at Henry M. Jackson Visitor Center and leads through flower fields to a prominent knoll overlooking Paradise, with views of Mount Adams and Mount St. Helens.

Dead Horse Creek Trail: This 2.5-mile spur trail joins the Skyline Trail below Glacier Vista. It is less steep than the Skyline Trail.

Golden Gate Trail: This trail is a variation of the Skyline Trail that reduces your trip by 1 mile. This hike offers views of wildflowers in Edith Creek Basin.

Mount Rainier seen from Snow Lake Trail.

Paradise Glacier Trail: This 6-mile round-trip hike begins in the Paradise parking area, crosses open flower meadows, and ends at a recently deglaciated moraine area just below Paradise Glacier.

Lakes Trail: This 5-mile loop takes you through subalpine meadows to Reflection Lakes, offering fine views of Stevens Ridge and the Tatoosh Range. The first part of the trail is the same as the Paradise Glacier Trail, starting by Paradise Inn. The trail climbs up to flowery Mazama Ridge, then descends into forest en route to the lakes.

Skyline Trail: This 5-mile loop trail, the highest trail at Paradise, begins by Paradise Inn. It takes you above tree line to Glacier Vista and Panorama Point for views of Mount Adams, Mount St. Helens, and the Nisqually Glacier.

Camp Muir: John Muir, founder of the Sierra Club and father of the national park system, was among an 1888 climbing party that made the sixth recorded ascent of the mountain. One of their campsites is now known as Camp Muir. This stone hut and level snow basin below Gibraltar Rock is used as a starting point for those planning to climb the mountain by the Ingraham Glacier route.

The 9-mile round-trip hike to Camp Muir, which lies at 10,000 feet, gains 4,600 feet. The hike begins by the Paradise ranger station and follows the Skyline Trail for 2.3 miles to Pebble Creek, where the Muir Snowfield begins. The next 2.2 miles involve an ascent of 2,800 feet up the snowfield. Caution is needed on this hike, since glaciers surround the Muir Snowfield. An error in navigation could put you onto a glacier with hidden crevasses.

Ohanapecosh Area

Grove of the Patriarchs Trail: This 1.3-mile round-trip nature trail is located just east of the Stevens Canyon Entrance Station. The hike follows the clear Ohanapecosh River to an island where there are 1,000-year-old western red cedar and Douglas fir of immense size.

Silver Falls Trail: This 3-mile round-trip loop is a low-elevation hike that's usually open early in the season. The trailhead lies at 1,950 feet elevation and begins and ends in the Ohanapecosh Campground at Loop B. The trail winds through a moss-laden old-growth forest along the clear-flowing Ohanapecosh River, passes the Ohanapecosh Hot Springs, and

Silver Falls on Ohanapecosh River.

follows the old boundary trail to Silver Falls, where the Ohanapecosh River falls 75 feet. There is a bridge at the falls, and the trail leads back to the campground on the opposite side of the river.

Shriner Peak Trail: This steep trail that gains 3,434 feet in 4 miles to the lookout on Shriner Peak is worth the effort. From the 5,834-foot summit, there are tremendous views of the Ohanapecosh Valley and Mount Rainier. The trailhead is located along the East Side Highway 3 miles from the Stevens Canyon entrance.

Tipsoo Lake/Chinook Pass Area

Naches Peak Loop: This 4.5-mile loop trail circles Naches Peak and provides hikers with spectacular views of Mount Rainier. The trail is best started off State Route 410 at Chinook Pass, ending at Tipsoo Lake, where you can walk back up the highway to the starting point. The trailhead is at 5,040 feet and is usually snowfree only after mid-July. You first follow the Pacific Crest Trail, passing out of Mount Rainier National Park and into the William O. Douglas Wilderness. Wildflowers are abundant in midsummer, and in late summer and fall, there is an abundance of huckleberries.

White River Area

Glacier Basin Trail: This 7-mile round-trip hike follows an old mining road for the first 2 miles, then climbs some switchbacks into the flowery Glacier Basin. There are some ruins of the old Storbo Copper Mine near the upper end of the trail. The trailhead is located at the upper end of the White River Campground. After the first mile, there is an 0.5-mile side trail that leads to a view of the rubble-covered Emmons Glacier, the largest glacier in the lower forty-eight. Watch for mountain goats on the surrounding slopes and for mountain climbers ascending the Inter Glacier to Camp Schurman.

Crystal Lakes Trail: This 6-mile round-trip hike to Lower Crystal Lake climbs through the forest on a series of switchbacks that provide a good look at Mount Rainier until the view is eclipsed by Crystal Peak. The next mile leads to forested Lower Crystal Lake, the smaller of the two lakes. The lovely open basin containing Upper Crystal Lake lies 0.5 mile beyond the lower lake. The trailhead is located on the east side of State Route 410 near Crystal Creek, about 4 miles north of Cayuse Pass toward the north park boundary.

The rocky slopes above Summerland and Frying Pan Creek are some of the best places in the park to see mountain goats.

Summerland Trail: This lovely 8.5-mile round-trip hike takes you to a green meadow basin below Little Tahoma. The first part of the hike is through old-growth forest. After crossing Frying Pan Creek, a glacial stream, ascend some switchbacks to a stone shelter and campsites. The trailhead is just beyond the Frying Pan Creek bridge, 3 miles from the White River Entrance Station.

Sunrise Area

Sourdough Ridge Nature Trail: This short, 1-mile round-trip trail begins at the Sunrise parking area and ascends to Sourdough Ridge through beautiful subalpine meadows. From the ridge, there are breathtaking views of Mount Rainier, Mount Baker, Glacier Peak, and Mount Adams.

Mount Fremont Trail: This 5.5-mile round-trip hike starts from the Sunrise parking area. The trail ascends 800 feet, first climbing up Sourdough Ridge, which you follow to Frozen Lake, where there is a major trail junction. From this point, the trail climbs another ridgeline of Mount Fremont to a fire lookout on a spur ridge of the mountain. From the lookout, there are magnificent views of Mount Rainier and the Cascade Range to the north and east.

Shadow Lake Trail: Starting at the Sunrise parking area, this 3-mile round-trip trail descends a short distance to the rim overlooking the White River Valley, with great views of Mount Rainier. The trail drops to Shadow Lake, from which you can return to Sunrise on the old roadway or via the steeper trail to Frozen Lake and Sourdough Ridge.

Burroughs Mountain Trail: Burroughs Mountain, named for naturalist and essayist John Burroughs, is a remnant of an ancient lava flow that filled what was once a valley. The hard lava resisted subsequent erosion and is now elevated above the surrounding landscape. The 7-mile round-trip trail gains 900 feet in elevation, offering outstanding views of Mount Rainier. The trailhead is on the south side of the Sunrise parking area. The first part of the trail passes Shadow Lake, then climbs to an overlook of the White River and Emmons Glacier. Beyond the overlook, the route continues up and onto the wide, flat plateau of First Burroughs Mountain. Another 0.5 mile leads hikers to 7,400-foot Second Burroughs.

Burroughs Mountain near Sunrise is named for New York naturalist and writer John Burroughs.

Hikers by Mount Burroughs.

Carbon River Area

Carbon Glacier Trail: This 7-mile round-trip hike provides a close-up look at a glacier. The trail starts at the Ipsut Creek Campground and follows the Carbon River through the forest all the way to the snout of the glacier.

Tolmie Peak Trail: This 7-mile round-trip trail follows a gentle grade most of the way to a fire lookout with stunning views of Mount Rainier. From the Mowich Lake parking area, the trail passes through forest to Eunice Lake before climbing to the lookout.

Mowich Lake Area

Spray Park Trail: Spray Park often offers some of the best wildflower displays in the park. The 6-mile round-trip trail begins at Mowich Lake. The first part follows the Wonderland Trail, but the trail to Spray Park splits less than 0.25 mile from the trailhead and heads uphill through forest. At 1.5 miles you reach Spray Falls, a worthy destination in its own right. Continue upward, following switchbacks on the main trail, until you break out into open meadows and ridges, with spectacular views of Rainier on clear days.

Spray Falls.

Hikers in Spray Park. There are more than 300 miles of trail in the park.

Nisqually Area

Lake George and Gobblers Knob Lookout Trail: This is a 10-mile round-trip hike to Lake George, with another 3 miles round-trip to the top of Gobblers Knob, where there is a lookout with a magnificent view of Mount Rainier. A hike all the way to the lookout and back will take a full day. To find the trailhead, turn off the main park road onto the Westside Road 1 mile east of the Nisqually entrance. Follow the road 3 miles to a washout, where the hike begins. It is 4 gradual miles up the old road to Round Pass. From the pass, it is 1 more mile to Lake George, a half-mile-long lake popular for overnight camping. From the lake the trail is steep, climbing 1,500 feet to the fire lookout, with a grand view of Mount Rainier.

Longmire Area

Trail of the Shadows: This short 0.5-mile interpretive loop trail is across from the National Park Inn at Longmire and provides information on the meadows, plants, animals, and human history of the mineral springs that prompted James Longmire to build a lodge in the area.

Rampart Ridge Trail: This 4.6-mile loop gains 1,339 feet and provides excellent views of Longmire and the Nisqually Valley to the south, Mount Rainier to the north, and Mount Wow, Tumtum Peak, and the path of the Kautz Creek Mudflow of 1947 to the west. The Rampart Ridge Trail begins at the Trail of the Shadows. If you have the time and energy, and prearranged a pickup at Christine Falls, a longer loop can be hiked by continuing up Rampart Ridge to Van Trump Park, then returning via Comet Falls and Christine Falls.

Carter Falls Trail: This 2-mile round-trip hike passes through old-growth forest along the Paradise River. Walk past Carter Falls another 50 yards to see Madcap Falls. The trailhead is located 100 yards downhill from the Cougar Rock Campground entrance.

Lousewort.

Waterfall on Van Trump Creek. The creek is named for Philemon Van Trump, who, along with Hazard Stevens, was the first to climb Mount Rainier in 1870.

Van Trump Park and Comet Falls Trail: This 5-mile round-trip hike begins 4.4 miles uphill from Longmire. The steep trail climbs through forest to Comet Falls, the second highest falls in the park, at 320 feet. You can turn around here, but it's worth continuing to Van Trump Park, which offers close-up views of Mount Rainier from flower-studded meadows.

Eagle Peak Trail: This 7-mile round-trip hike from Longmire takes you to the saddle just below the summit of Eagle Peak. Most of the hike is an easy grade through forest, but the final 0.5 mile is steep and opens up to a rocky saddle that offers great views of Mount Rainier.

Wonderland Trail: The ultimate hiking trail in the park is the 93-mile-long Wonderland Trail, which encircles Mount Rainier, crossing alpine meadows, glacial streams, and mountain passes and penetrating valley forests. The trail traverses across the slopes of the mountain, ascending ridges that radiate out from Rainier's summit and descending into the intervening valleys, reaching a maximum elevation of 6,500 feet at Panhandle Gap. The views along the trail are tremendous. Most people allot ten days to hike the entire trail. Daily elevation gains and losses of over 3,500 feet are common.

Meadows at Paradise frame Mount Rainier's glaciers.

Nearby Areas

Clearwater Wilderness

The 14,300-acre Clearwater Wilderness lies north of the Carbon River in the Mount Baker-Snoqualmie National Forest. The wilderness sits at the headwaters of the Greenwater River and South Prairie Creek and hosts a dozen small lakes and magnificent forests. Elevations vary from 2,000 to 6,089 feet at the top of Bearhead Mountain, the highest point in the wilderness. The forest is typical of the west-side Cascades, dominated by Douglas fir and western hemlock. Black bear, elk, black-tailed deer, mountain lions, and bobcats have been reported for the area. A number of trails traverse the area. Trailheads are located off Forest Service roads in the White River and the Carbon River Valleys.

Norse Peak Wilderness

The 50,923-acre Norse Peak Wilderness is administratively split between the Wenatchee and Mount Baker-Snoqualmie National Forests. The wilderness lies on the eastern slope of the Cascades just east of Mount Rainier National Park. Chinook Pass and State Route 410 mark its southern limits. The highest summits are just under 7,000 feet in elevation. The area is extremely rugged, cut by deep river canyons of the Greenwater and Naches Rivers, and contains several dozen glaciated alpine lake basins.

The historic Naches Pass Trail, used by pioneers like James Longmire to cross the Cascades in 1853, lies just north of the wilderness. Some of the area was heavily prospected for gold and silver in the late 1800s, and old cabins and mine shafts can still be found.

A good network of trails provides hikers access throughout the area. Several roads and trailheads lie along State Route 410, both north and east of Mount Rainier National Park.

Glacier View Wilderness

The Glacier View Wilderness lies within the Gifford Pinchot National Forest. Though a mere 3,080 acres, its immediate proximity to Mount Rainier National Park's western border makes it part of a larger roadless complex. The wilderness has been glaciated in the past, and there are nine small alpine lakes and meadows at the headwaters of the South Fork of Puyallup River. The higher ridges in the wilderness provide great views of Rainier. In the late summer, the abundance of ripe huckleberries lures the hiker off the trail.

The wilderness is accessed by Forest Service Road 59 off State Route 706 between Ashford and the Mount Rainier Park boundary. There are a number of trails, some of which take the hiker to Gobblers Knob lookout and Lake George in Mount Rainier National Park.

Tatoosh Wilderness

Looking south from Paradise Meadows, the rugged peaks visible are part of the Tatoosh Range. Some of these peaks are within Mount Rainier National Park, but the southern part of the range is located within the 15,800-acre Tatoosh Wilderness, which is administered by the Gifford Pinchot National Forest. The lower portion of this range is heavily forested, but the higher elevations have been glaciated into rugged, sawtooth peaks. Elevations range from 1,200 to 6,310 feet. There is only one trail in the wilderness, accessible from Forest Service Road 52.

William O. Douglas Wilderness

The 167,195-acre William O. Douglas Wilderness, administered by the Gifford Pinchot and Wenatchee National Forests, is named for the Supreme Court justice and conservationist, who had a cabin at Goose Prairie and spent many years hiking in this wilderness. Drained by the Bumping River, the wilderness, which sprawls across the Cascades just east of Mount Rainier National Park, has fifty-nine lakes scattered across a subalpine plateau. Many of the area's glacial cirque basins contain subalpine meadows that are grazed extensively by sheep, and the area also supports large herds of mule deer and elk. The wilderness is accessed by more than 250 miles of trails, including a portion of the Pacific Crest Trail. Numerous trailheads are scattered along U.S. 12 and State Route 410.

Flowers along the Pacific Crest Trail in the William O. Douglas Wilderness frame Mount Rainier. William Douglas was a Supreme Court justice and outspoken wilderness advocate.

Federation Forest

The Federation Forest is a 619-acre state park 16 miles southeast of Enumclaw along State Route 410. It is a showcase of old-growth forest, with some of the largest western red cedar in the state. There are several nature trails, an interpretative center, and a picnic area.

Crystal Mountain Ski Resort

Crystal Mountain is a winter sports center located on the northeast border of Mount Rainier Park. In summer, the area offers a high-speed chair lift to the top of Crystal Mountain, providing a 7,000-foot vantage point with terrific views of Mount Rainier. The turn-off for the resort is located on State Route 410, just north of the White River entrance to Mount Rainier National Park.

CHECKLIST OF MOUNT RAINIER BIRDS

This list includes all species recorded for Mount Rainier. Many are seen only during migration, and some species are very rare or accidental. Abundance for many species varies considerably throughout the year. Ratings are for summer abundance, or if found in Rainier only during migration, then occurrence at that time. Ratings assume one is looking in the appropriate habitat and season for that species.

Rating scales

A	abundant	O	occasional
C	common	R	rare
UC	uncommon		

Loons
___ Common loon
  (*Gavia immer*) R

Grebes
___ Western grebe
  (*Aechmophorus occidentalis*) R

Herons
___ Great blue heron
  (*Ardea herodias*) UC

Geese and Ducks
___ Canada goose
  (*Branta canadensis*) R
___ Green-winged teal
  (*Anas crecca*) O
___ Mallard
  (*Anas platyrhynchos*) O
___ Northern pintail
  (*Anas acuta*) R
___ Harlequin duck
  (*Histrionicus histrionicus*) O

INDEX

Page numbers in italics indicate illustrations.